AF593165

GENERAL ORDERS
SPAIN AND PORTUGAL

JANUARY 2ND TO DECEMBER 29TH, 1810

VOLUME II.

SPAIN AND PORTUGAL

1810

A photographic reproduction of the original edition printed in London, 1811, by T. Egerton.

2022
Waterville, Maine
pagesofpages.com

ISBN: 979-8-9855566-3-6 (Wrappers)

INTRODUCTION TO VOLUME TWO

This is the second volume of the General Orders issued by direction of Arthur Wellesley, commander of the allied forces in the Peninsula. It spans the year 1810, which was – in terms of major battles – the quietest period for British forces until after the Battle of Waterloo. The major battle of the year, under Wellington's command, was the Battle of Bussaco (or Busaco, as it is spelled in this volume). There is a brief complimentary notice of the battle in pages for September 30th, 1810, immediately followed by a rare pardon of four soldiers, condemned to be hung for robbing "some Portuguese inhabitant or inhabitants on or about the 12th of March, 1810". The pardon was due to the gallantry displayed by the 25th regiment on the 27th.

A substantial portion of this volume is given over to the reports of general courts martial, and not many common soldiers escaped – typical sentences are to be hung, or shot, or given some quantity of lashes from 500 to 1200, or transportation. Officers made out much better, with generally the severest punishment being cashiering.

The complete list of the volumes of General Orders is given on the next page.

Vol	Pub Date	Contents	Title Variations
1	1811	April 27th - Dec 28th, 1809	General Orders. Spain and Portugal. Volume I. London: Printed by Authority by T. Egerton
2	1812	January 2nd to December 29th, 1810.	General Orders. Spain and Portugal. Volume II. London: Printed by Authority by T. Egerton
3	1811	January 1st to December 31st, 1811.	General Orders. Spain and Portugal. Volume II. London: Printed by Authority by T. Egerton
4	1813	January 1st to December 30th, 1812.	General Orders. Spain and Portugal. Volume IV. London: Printed by Authority by T. Egerton
5	1814	January 7th to December 28th, 1813.	General Orders. Spain and France. Volume V. London: Printed by Authority by T. Egerton
6	1817	1814	General Orders. France, 1814. Volume VI. to which is added a general alphabetical index for the orders of 1809, 1810, 1811 & 1812. London.
7	1815	April 11 to December 31st, 1815.	General Orders. Flanders and France. Volume VII. Paris: Military Press.
8	186?	1816	General Orders. France, 1816.Volume VIII. Cambrai.
9	1816	1817	General Orders. France, 1817. Volume IX. 206 p. [Cambrai.] Printed at the Head Quarters of the Army [by Serjeant Buchan 3rd. Foot Guards]1817.
10	1816	1818	General Orders. France, 1818. Volume X. Cambrai.

GENERAL ORDERS.

SPAIN AND PORTUGAL.

JANUARY 2ND TO DECEMBER 29TH,

1810.

VOL. II.

LONDON.

Printed by Authority,

BY T. EGERTON, MILITARY LIBRARY, WHITEHALL.

1811.

G. O.

Adjutant General's Office
Pombal, 2d Jan. 1810.

1. Major General Lightburne's brigade, consisting of the 2d battalion 5th and 58th regiments, will form a part of the 4th division of Infantry.

2. Major the Hon. J. Ponsonby, 23d Light Dragoons, is appointed to act as an Assistant in the Adjutant General's department, till his Majesty's pleasure is known.

3. Ensign Green, 83d regiment, will place himself under the orders of Marshal Beresford.

G. O.

Adjutant General's Office.
Coimbra, 3d Jan. 1810.

1. Head-quarters are for the present at Coimbra; they will be moved to Vizeu in a few days.

2. The Paymasters of the regiments in Lieutenant General Sir John Sherbrooke's, the 3d and 4th divisions of Infantry and the Hussars, are to send to Coimbra as soon as they please for the balances due on their estimates, to the 24th December.

ADJUTANT GENERAL'S OFFICE.

G. O. *Coimbra, 4th Jan.* 1810.

PAYMASTERS of the regiments in Lieutenant General Hill's division of Infantry, in Major General Slade's, Brigadier General Fane's, and Brigadier General Anson's brigade of Cavalry, are to proceed to Santarem, where they will find a person belonging to the Paymaster General's department, who will pay them the balances due on their estimates, to the 24th December.

ADJUTANT GENERAL'S OFFICE.

G. A. O. *Coimbra, 5th Jan.* 1810.

1. As the profession of Free Masonry is contrary to the law of Portugal, the Commander of the Forces requests that the meetings of the lodges existing in the several corps, the use of masonic badges and emblems, and the appearances of the Officers and soldiers in masonic processions may be discontinued, while the troops will be in this country.

The Commander of the Forces is convinced, that the Officers and soldiers of the army will feel the necessity of obeying the laws of the country which they are sent to protect, and that they will shew their respect for the attachment of the people of Portugal to their own laws, by refraining from an amusement which, however innocent in itself, and allowed by the law of Great Britain, is a violation of the law of this country, and very disagreeable to the people.

2. The Officers of the army are informed, that the Government of Portugal have lately issued a decree, by which

which they have called upon all persons having horses of a description fit for the Portuguese Cavalry, to send them to certain depôts formed for their reception, without loss of time; and as the Government have been informed, that some of the horse dealers and others, have offered their horses for sale to the Officers of the British army;

The Commander of the Forces wishes to warn the Officers of the army, those persons who shall thus dispose of them, will be guilty of a breach of the law of the country; and that the purchasers of the horses of this description, after the date of the decree in question, will be liable to lose the horses they shall have purchased.

Horses fit for cavalry service are fifteen hands.

ADJUTANT GENERAL'S OFFICE.

G. A. O. *Coimbra, 6th Jan.* 1810.

MR. Deputy Commissary General Rawlings is to place himself under the orders of the Commissary General of the British army.

The Officers of the Staff will be paid to the 24th December, on application to the Paymaster General.

ADJUTANT GENERAL'S OFFICE.

G. O. *Coimbra, 9th Jan.* 1810.

HEAD-QUARTERS will move to-morrow by the annexed route.

January 10th	. . . .	Mealhada
Do. 11th	. . . .	St. Combadaõ
Do. 12th	. . . .	Vizeu

 G. O.

ADJUTANT GENERAL'S OFFICE.

G. O. *Vizeu, 12th Jan.* 1810.

1. ALL Officers wishing to go to any part of the country by post, must apply for a passport; if at head-quarters to the Commander of the Forces; if at any of the cantonments of the army, or at Lisbon, Elvas, &c., to the General Officer commanding the division, or to the Commanding Officer at Lisbon, Elvas, &c. respectively; to whom blank passports will be transmitted for this purpose.

2. When the Commissary, attached to any division detached from head-quarters, wishes to send a courier by post, he is to apply to the Commanding Officer of the division for a passport, who will grant it if he should concur in the expediency of sending the courier.

The Commissary General will apply for passports for the same purpose to the Commander of the Forces.

3. Persons belonging to the English army will not be supplied with post horses at any of the post stages, unless they should produce these passports for post horses of the Commander of the Forces.

4. When soldiers are sent to the general, or any detachment hospital, their ammunition is to be delivered into store to the Officer commanding the artillery, with the division in which the regiment is placed, with a return of the quantity so delivered in; which the Officer commanding the artillery with the division is to direct the Commissary of artillery to receive. The Commanding Officers of regiments are to adopt means for the preservation of the ammunition of soldiers iu regimental hospitals.

5. The Commander of the Forces desires that the shooting of bullocks may be discontinued, as being a great waste of ammunition.

6. The

6. The Government of Portugal having expressed their desire to give the troops a double allowance of wine on three days, as a demonstration of their satisfaction; upon the return of the army to Portugal, a double allowance for each man is to be issued by the Commissary, on the 18th instant, being her Majesty's birth-day, on the 21st of January, and on the 28th of January.

7. The Officers commanding regiments are informed, that they must not allow either Officers or soldiers to absent themselves from their regiments without leave from the Commander of the Forces.

ADJUTANT GENERAL'S OFFICE.

G. O. *Vizeu, 16th Jan.* 1810.

Memorandum—TILL further orders, instead of Thursday, the army mail for England will be closed at 2 o'clock on each Wednesday, and will be dispatched immediately after from head-quarters.

ADJUTANT GENERAL'S OFFICE.

G. O. *Vizeu, 23d Jan.* 1810.

LIEUTENANT C. Bayly, 31st regiment, is appointed to act as a Deputy Assistant in the Adjutant General's department, till his Majesty's pleasure is known.

Lieutenant Bayley is attached to the 2d division of Infantry.

ADJUTANT GENERAL'S OFFICE.

G. A. O. *Vizeu, 23d Jan.* 1810.

THE Commander of the Forces desires that the Brigade Major, of Major General Lightburne's brigade, will send to the Adjutant General, of the 4th division, a return, stating the dates and numbers of the several General Orders received by that brigade; which the Assistant Adjutant General will examine, and he will send to the brigade any General Orders which they may not already have received.

The Commander of the Forces desires the attention of Major General Lightburne to all these orders.

ADJUTANT GENERAL'S OFFICE.

G. O. *Vizeu, 24th Jan.* 1810.

1. AT a General Court Martial, held by virtue and in pursuance of an order from his Excellency Lord Viscount Wellington, Lisbon, December 27th, 1809, were arraigned Corporal Wm. Hammond, Privates Arthur M'Cannagh and Stephen Hudson, of the 84th regiment, on the following charges, viz.

First Charge.

Having whilst on duty over the army baggage stores in Lisbon, during the night of the 30th November, or morning of the 1st December, 1809, conspired to break open the said stores.

Second Charge.

For having broken open the said stores whilst on duty as a safeguard thereon.

Third

Third Charge.

Having stolen from the said stores, several articles belonging to the different regiments of the army.

Fourth Charge.

For absenting themselves from their post when on duty over the said army baggage stores, and drinking in a wine house contiguous thereto.

Opinion and Sentence.

The Court having duly weighed and considered the evidences against the prisoners, Lance Corporal William Hammond, privates Arthur M'Cannagh and Stephen Hudson, of the 87th regiment of foot, with what they have urged in their defence, are of opinion that they are guilty of the whole of the charges brought against them, in breach of the Articles of War, viz.

1st, For having whilst on duty over the army baggage stores at Lisbon, during the night of the 30th November, or morning of the 1st December, conspired to break open the said stores.

2d, For having broken open the said stores whilst on duty thereon.

3d, Having stolen from the said stores several articles belonging to the different regiments of the army.

4th, For absenting themselves from their post when on duty over the said army baggage stores, and drinking in a wine house contiguous thereto.

The Court do adjudge the prisoner Lance Corporal William Hammond, 87th regiment of foot, to be shot to death; at such time and place as his Excellency the Commander of the Forces may please to direct.

The Court also do adjudge the prisoners Arthur M'Cannagh and Stephen Hudson, privates in the 87th regiment of foot, to receive each 1200 lashes, in the usual manner, at such time and place as his Excellency the Commander of the Forces may please to direct.

Which sentence has been confirmed by his Excellency the Commander of the Forces.

The sentence of the General Court Martial on Corporal William Hammond, Arthur M'Cannagh, and Stephen Hudson, of the 87th regiment, is to be carried into execution in the afternoon on Monday next, by the Assistant Provost at Lisbon, in presence of the troops under arms composing the garrison of Lisbon.

2. The General Court Martial, of which Colonel Peacocke is President, is dissolved; and the members are to return to their duty.

3. A General Court Martial will assemble at Vizeu, on Thursday the 25th of January, at 11 o'clock, for the trial of such prisoners as may be brought before it.

Colonel the Hon. Edward Stopford, President.

	Field Officers.	Captains.	Subalterns.
Royal Artillery	1 —	0 —	1
1st Division of Infantry	3 —	6 —	3
Total . .	4 —	6 —	4

Names and dates of commissions of the members, and list of evidences, to be sent in by this evening, to the Adjutant General's Office, directed to the Deputy Judge Advocate.

All evidences to be warned to attend.

G. A. O.

ADJUTANT GENERAL'S OFFICE,

G. A. O. *Vizeu, 24th Jan.* 1810.

1. A GENERAL Court Martial will assemble at Abrantes, on Monday the 29th of January, for the trial of such prisoners as may be brought before it.

Brigadier General R. Stewart, President.

Members to be furnished by the 2d division of Infantry.

2. The Paymaster General will issue to the Paymasters of regiments the balances due on their estimates to this day.

To those of the 3d and 4th divisions, and of the Hussars, as soon as the Paymasters of those regiments shall come in, and to those of Lieutenant General Sherbrook's division; after those at the further cantonments will have received their money—notice will be given, when the latter are to attend for payment.

3. As the distance which the army is from Lisbon, makes it impossible to procure money in time to discharge the amount of the estimates in advance as required by the regulations, and as the consequence of the discharge of the balances due to the soldiers on the 24th of each month, for the month then ending, would be, that for a month the Officers commanding companies would have no money in hand to supply those necessaries which the soldiers should require;

The Commander of the Forces desires that in future the accounts of the soldiers are to be settled on the 24th of every month, according to the regulations of the service and the balances struck, but the balance is not to be paid to the soldiers till the 24th of the following month; that is to say, the balance due to the soldiers on the 24th of of January not till the 24th of February, and thus in succession from month to month.

An alteration in conformity to this order must be made in the certificate of payment at the bottom of the monthly return of regiments.

ADJUTANT GENERAL'S OFFICE.
G. O. *Vizeu, 25th Jan.* 1810.

THE Officers commanding regiments are requested to make a return to the Adjutant General, as soon as possible, stating what sums of money have been stopt from the soldiers for cartridges lost.

ADJUTANT GENERAL'S OFFICE.
G. O. *Vizeu, 27th Jan.* 1810.

1. HOSPITAL Mate Rosa is appointed to act as an Assistant Surgeon to the 16th Light Dragoons till his Majesty's pleasure is known.

2. The following notifications of promotions have been received:

Martin Lima, Gent. to be Ensign in the 48th Regiment, bearing date 17th August, 1809.

G. A. O.

ADJUTANT GENERAL'S OFFICE.

G. A. O. *Vizeu, 27th Jan.* 1810.

THE passports for post-horses sent to the Officers commanding divisions, &c. are to be used only to procure post-horses for couriers and others whom it may be necessary to send by post upon the public service, or for Officers to whom the Officers in whose hands the passports are lodged chuse to give permission to travel by post.

ADJUTANT GENERAL'S OFFICE.

G. O. *Vizeu, 28th Jan.* 1810.

LIEUTENANT Dundas, 2d battalion 5th Regiment, is to act as Brigade Major to Major General Lightburn's brigade of Infantry during the absence of Brigade Major Potter on account of indisposition.

ADJUTANT GENERAL'S OFFICE.

G. A. O. *Vizeu, 28th Jan.* 1810.

THE Commander of the Forces is desirous that all men who are sick and require carriage should be removed to the General Hospital established at Coimbra from the several cantonments of the army once a week, according to arrangements and directions sent by the Quarter-Master General and Inspector of Hospitals to the Officers of the Quarter-Master General's department, and Medical Staff attached to the different divisions of the army.

The

The General Officers are requested to see those directions, and have them carried into execution.

G. O.

Adjutant General's Office.
Vizeu, 29th Jan. 1810.

A confirmation of the following promotions in the Medical department has been received:

Surgeon M. A. Burmeister, 66th Regiment, to be Surgeon to the Forces.

Surgeon George Guthrie, 29th Regiment, to be Surgeon to the Forces.

14th Light Dragoons.

Hospital Mate George Lardner to be Assistant Surgeon, vice M'Gillivray promoted in the 60th Foot.

3d Regiment of Foot or Buffs.

Hospital Mate Frederick Brown to be Assistant Surgeon, vice Stainford promoted to the 29th Foot.

9th Foot.

Hospital Mate Thomas Tidder to be Assistant Surgeon, vice Miles deceased.

29th Foot.

Assistant Surgeon J. E. Stainford, from the 3d Foot, to be Surgeon, vice Guthrie promoted to the Staff.

40*th*

40*th Foot.*

Hospital Mate William Barry to be Assistant Surgeon, vice Forcade promoted to the 83d Foot.

48*th Foot.*

Hospital Mate William Moffatt to be Assistant Surgeon.

57*th Foot.*

Hospital Mate C. Humphreys to be Assistant Surgeon, vice Warsdell, in the 66th Regiment.

Hospital Mate Thomas Snow to be Assistant Surgeon.

60*th Foot.*

Assistant Surgeon G. Beattie, from the 92d Regiment, to be Surgeon, vice M'Gillivray, deceased.

66*th Foot.*

Assistant Surgeon Warsdell, from the 57th Regiment, to be Surgeon, vice Burmeister promoted on the Staff.

83*d Foot.*

Assistant Surgeon H. Forcade, from 40th Regiment, to be Surgeon, vice Bruff promoted on the Staff.

ADJUTANT GENERAL'S OFFICE.

G. A. O. *Vizeu, 29th Jan.* 1810.

THE General Court Martial, of which Colonel Warren Peacocke was President, and the under-mentioned Officers

Officers were members, held at Lisbon, on Monday, 27th November, 1809, and for the trial of Edward Poole, Civilian, and follower of the army, will re-assemble at Lisbon on the 8th day of February next.

Colonel G. De Grey, 1st Dragoons.
Lieutenant Colonel Maister, 34th Regiment.
Major Gwyn, 45th Regiment.
Major Gough, 87th Regiment.
Major Jervois, 1st Dragoons.
Major Aird, Royal Waggon Train.
Captain Purvis, 1st Dragoons.
Captain M'Mahon, 5th battalion 60th Regiment.
Captain Montague, 1st Dragoons.
Captain Milne, 45th Regiment.
Captain T. Tuckett, 3d or Buffs.
Captain Mansergh, 83d Regiment.
Captain William Crosbie, 1st Dragoons.
Captain Hon. H. Powys, 83d Regiment.
Lieutenant Crompton, 9th Foot, A. D. Judge Advocate.

ADJUTANT GENERAL'S OFFICE.
G. O. *Vizeu, 30th Jan.* 1810.

1. AT a General Court Martial, held by virtue of a warrant, and in pursuance of an order from his Excellency Lord Viscount Wellington, whereof Colonel the Hon. Edward Stopford was President, was arraigned Private George Sasson, third class, Royal Staff Corps, on the following charges, viz.

FIRST

FIRST CHARGE.

For having entered the room of Philippa, a Portuguese woman, which was in the house of Margaritta Candida de Jesus, after tattoo, on the night of the 22d instant, and having behaved in a most disorderly manner.

SECOND CHARGE.

For attempting to force into the said room, between the hours of 10 and 11, after having been turned out of the house; and not having been able to force the door, for having clandestinely entered the house of Margaritta Candida de Jesus, by the upper window.

THIRD CHARGE.

For having assaulted and attempted to commit a rape on the body of Philippa, a Portuguese woman, and having used other violence supposed to have caused her death.

To which charge the prisoner, Private George Sasson, of the Royal Staff Corps, pleaded not guilty, and the Court proceeded to the examination of evidences.

OPINION AND SENTENCE.

The Court having maturely and deliberately weighed and considered the evidence adduced on the part of the prosecution, as well as that which the prisoner, Private George Sasson, Royal Staff Corps, has urged in his defence, are of opinion that a part of the 1st charge is proved against the prisoner, Private George Sasson, Royal Staff Corps, viz. Being in the house of Margaritta Candida de Jesus, after hours, on the night of the 22d instant;

stant; but do acquit him of guilt thereof, in consequence of his acting under the immediate orders of his master, Lieutenant Freeth, Royal Staff Corps; and there being no proof of the prisoner having behaved in a most disorderly manner, as specified in the latter part of the 1st charge, they do acquit him thereof.

The Court do acquit the prisoner, Private George Sasson, Royal Staff Corps, of the 2d and 3d charges.

The Court cannot close its proceedings without noticing the extreme impropriety of conduct of Lieutenant Freeth, Royal Staff Corps, in sending the prisoner his servant out after hours, knowing him to be drunk, which was the cause of his being brought before a General Court Martial, and his being tried for a capital offence; which decision has been confirmed by his Excellency the Commander of the Forces.

2. The Officers of the army who have soldiers for their servants, should be particularly cautious not to give them orders, the execution of which are breaches of discipline and good order, and not to expose them in a state of intoxication to the temptation of committing offences, which must lead to the punishment of the soldier.

ADJUTANT GENERAL'S OFFICE.

G. A. O. *Vizeu*, 31*st Jan.* 1810.

1. As the produce of straw in this country is but small, the ration is to be reduced from 14 lbs. to 10 lbs. for each horse or mule, and that of Indian corn or barley increased to 12 lbs.

2. The

2. The 1st and 3d Dragoon Guards, 4th, 14th, and 16th Dragoons, and the Hussars, are to continue to receive the ration as usual.

ADJUTANT GENERAL'S OFFICE.

G. A. O. *Vizeu, 2d Feb.* 1810.

THE Paymasters of the 1st division of the army will receive the balances due on their estimates to the 24th January, on Saturday the 3d instant.

ADJUTANT GENERAL'S OFFICE.

G. O. *Vizeu, 4th Feb.* 1810.

Memorandum—THE General Court Martial, of which Colonel the Honourable Edward Stopford is President, ordered to meet on Monday the 5th instant, is not to reassemble till Thursday the 8th February, at 11 o'clock.

ADJUTANT GENERAL'S OFFICE.

G. O. *Vizeu, 14th Feb.* 1810.

HOSPITAL Mate Henry Retford is appointed to act as an Assistant Surgeon to the 45th Regiment till his Majesty's pleasure is known, vice Chambers absent without leave.

ADJUTANT GENERAL'S OFFICE.

G. O. *Vizeu*, 18*th Feb.* 1810.

1. AT a General Court Martial held by virtue of a warrant, and in pursuance of an order from his Excellency Lord Viscount Wellington, held at Abrantes, February 2d, 1810, was arraigned Patrick Lang and John Welby, privates in the 1st battalion 3d Regiment, or Buffs, on the following charges:

FIRST CHARGE.

For unsoldierlike conduct in being out of their quarters after hours on the night of the 6th January, and, on returning to their quarters at an unseasonable hour, behaving in a riotous and disorderly manner.

SECOND CHARGE.

For ill-treating De Castres, a Portuguese woman, in their quarters, by throwing her down stairs, which act of violence caused her death.

OPINION.

The Court having considered the evidences against the prisoners, John Welby and Patrick Lang, were of opinion they are not guilty of the charges exhibited against them, and do therefore acquit them; which decision has been confirmed by his Excellency the Commander of the Forces.

2. Lieutenant Pemberton, 95th Regiment, is appointed to act as Aide-de-Camp to Brigadier General Campbell till his Majesty's pleasure is known.

This

This appointment is to bear date from the 25th August last, when Lieutenant Pemberton joined the Brigadier General.

3. Captain the Honourable James Stewart, 95th Regiment, is appointed to act as Brigade Major till his Majesty's pleasure is known, to the brigade of Infantry under the command of Major General the Honourable William Stewart.

G. O.

ADJUTANT GENERAL'S OFFICE.
Vizeu, 19*th Feb.* 1810.

1. AT a General Court Martial assembled by virtue of a warrant, and in pursuance of an order from his Excellency Lord Viscount Wellington, whereof Colonel the Honourable Edward Stopford was President, and Captain Goodman, Deputy Judge Advocate, held at Vizeu, February the 8th, 1810, was arraigned John Benderman, Frederick Shoemaker, and Emanuel Kemp, private soldiers in the 1st battalion 11th Regiment, for desertion on or about the 17th day of December, 1809, to which charges the prisoners pleaded not guilty.

OPINION AND SENTENCE.

The Court having maturely and deliberately considered and weighed the evidence adduced in support of the prosecution against the prisoners, John Benderman, Frederick Shoemaker, and Emanuel Kemp, private soldiers in the 1st battalion 11th Regiment, together with what they have offered in their defence, are of opinion they are guilty of the charge preferred against them, being a breach of the

Articles of War, and do by virtue thereof sentence them the prisoners, John Benderman, Frederick Shoemaker, and Emanuel Kemp, private soldiers in the 1st battalion 11th Regiment, to receive a punishment of 800 Lashes each, at such time and place as his Excellency the Commander of the Forces may deem fit; which sentence has been confirmed by his Excellency the Commander of the Forces.

In consequence however of the recommendation of the General Court Martial, the punishment awarded to John Benderman, Frederick Shoemaker, and Emanuel Kemp, is remitted, and they are to join their corps.

2. Captain Lord Clinton, 16th Light Dragoons, is appointed an extra Aide-de-Camp to the Commander of the Forces.

3. Captain Oliver Anderson, Royal Fusileers, is appointed to act as Deputy Assistant in the Quarter-Master General's department till his Majesty's pleasure is known.

4. Captain Rolt, 2d battalion 58th Regiment, will put himself under the orders of Marshal Beresford.

5. The following General Officers have been appointed to the Staff of this army.

Major General Thomas Picton.

Aide-de-Camp Captain Sir Orford Gordon.

Major General Honourable William Stewart.

Aide-de-Camp Captain R. B. Gabriel, 2d D. G.

G. A. O.

ADJUTANT GENERAL'S OFFICE.
Vizeu, 19*th Feb*. 1810.

1. THE dragoons belonging to the depôt squadrons now with the different regiments of Dragoon Guards and Dragoons are to be sent to Lisbon without loss of time; those belonging to Major General Slade's brigade by route from the Assistant Quarter-Master General, with Lieutenant General Hill's division; those belonging to Brigadier General Fane's brigade by route from the Assistant Quarter-Master General, with the Cavalry; and those of the 16th Light Dragoons by route from the Quarter-Master General.

Colonel Peacocke will report when these men shall have arrived at Lisbon.

2. During the absence from the army of Lieutenant Colonel Bathurst, all applications and letters hitherto addressed to the Military Secretary are to be sent to Captain Bouverie or Lord Fitzroy Somerset, and answers will be given by one of those Officers.

The warrants signed by the Commander of the Forces are to be countersigned by Captain Bouverie or Lord Fitzroy Somerset, and either of those Officers will sign the Duplicate and Triplicates to be lodged with the Commissary General.

G. O.

ADJUTANT GENERAL'S OFFICE.
Vizeu, 20*th Feb*. 1810.

1. CAPTAIN Baron Tripp, of the 11th Regiment, is appointed on the Staff of this army as a Deputy Assistant Adjutant General, to bear date from the 10th January.

2. Hospital Mate Thomas Hoey to be Assistant Surgeon to the Royal Waggon Train, vice Vassal promoted, till his Majesty's pleasure is known.

ADJUTANT GENERAL'S OFFICE,
G. A. O. *Vizeu, 20th Feb.* 1810.

THE General Court Martial ordered to re-assemble at Lisbon on the 8th day of February, and whereof Colonel Peacocke is President, is adjourned, and the members are to return to their duty.

ADJUTANT GENERAL'S OFFICE.
G. A. O. *Vizeu, 20th Feb.* 1810.

1. AT a General Court Martial held by virtue of a warrant, and in pursuance of an order from his Excellency Lord Viscount Wellington, whereof Colonel the Honourable Edward Stopford is President, and Captain Cockburne, Acting Deputy Judge Advocate, at Vizeu, 30th January, 1810, was arraigned Private James Overill, 61st Regiment, on the following charges:

FIRST CHARGE.

For having absented himself from his detachment without leave, by falling in rear of the escort to which he belonged, on the march between Pombal and Condeixa, on the 13th instant.

SECOND

SECOND CHARGE.

For having shot with his musket, and dangerously wounded, a Portuguese peasant, on the road from Pombal to Condeixa, on the 13th instant. To which charges the prisoner, James Overill, private in the 61st Regiment, pleaded not guilty, and the Court proceeded to the examination of evidences.

OPINION AND SENTENCE.

The Court having maturely weighed and considered the evidence brought forward in support of the prosecution as well as what the prisoner has urged in his defence, is of opinion that he, the prisoner Private James Overill, 61st Regiment, is guilty of the first charge preferred against him, viz. For having absented himself from his detachment without leave by falling in rear of the escort to which he belonged, on the march between Pombal and Condeixa, on the 13th instant, being in breach of the 5th article of the 14th Section of the Articles of War. The Court are further of opinion that the prisoner, Private James Overill, 61st Regiment, is guilty of the second charge preferred against him, viz. Having shot with his musket, and dangerously wounded, a Portuguese peasant, on the road from Pombal to Condeixa, on the 13th instant, being in breach of the 4th article of the 24th Section of the Articles of War, and do by virtue of the said articles sentence him the prisoner, Private James Overill, 61st Regiment, to receive a punishment of 1200 Lashes, at such time and place as his Excellency the Commander of the Forces shall direct; which sentence has been confirmed by his Excellency the Commander of the Forces.

Private James Overill, 61st Regiment, is to be sent to his regiment by the Provost Marshal, and the sentence of the General Court Martial is to be carried into execution on the 22d instant, under the direction of the Assistant Provost Marshal to the 1st division of Infantry, in presence of the brigade, under the command of Brigadier General Cameron, on parade.

2. The Paymaster General will make an advance to each of the regiments of 1500 dollars on account of their estimates to the 24th instant. The Paymasters of regiments in the 3d and 4th divisions, and the Hussars, will receive this money at Celorico on the 23d instant; the Paymasters of the regiments in the 1st division will send to Vizeu for it.

ADJUTANT GENERAL'S OFFICE.

G. O. *Vizeu, 22d Feb.* 1810.

1. THE brigade consisting of the 3d battalion 27th, 97th, and 40th Regiments, is to be Major General Cole's brigade; and that consisting of the 45th, 88th, and 74th Regiments, Major General Picton's.

2. The 3d division is to consist of the brigades of Major General Picton and Major General Lightburne; the 4th division, of the brigades of Major General Cole and Brigadier General Alexander Campbell: Major General Picton is to command the 3d division, and Major General Cole the 4th division, until further orders.

Colonel Kemmis is attached as a Colonel on the Staff to the brigade of the Honourable Major General Cole, and Colonel M'Kinnon as a Colonel on the Staff to the brigade

brigade of Major General Picton, during the time those Officers will command the 3d and 4th divisions respectively.

The Portuguese brigade of infantry, consisting of the 9th and 21st Regiments, now stationed at Coimbra, is attached to the 3d division; and the Portuguese brigade of infantry, consisting of the 3d and 15th Regiments, now stationed at Lamego, is attached to the 4th division. These brigades will hereafter be ordered to join the divisions to which they belong.

3. The 1st and 2d battalions of Portuguese Chasseurs are attached to the brigade of Brigadier General R. Craufurd, which is to be called the light division. These troops will be ordered to join the division to which they belong.

4. A company 5th battalion 60th Regiment is to be attached to each of the brigades of the army according to the plan detailed in the Orders of the 4th May, 1809. The Commanding Officer of the 5th battalion 60th Regiment will detach three companies to Lieutenant General Hill's division as soon as he shall receive this order, and a route from the Quarter-Master General for the purpose; and as the General Officers commanding brigades have invariably expressed the highest satisfaction with the uniform good conduct of this valuable body of men, which has always continued effective under many trying circumstances, the Commander of the Forces desires that as far as possible the same companies may be attached as formerly to the same brigades.

Two companies to be attached to Sir John Sherbrook's division, one to the brigade of Guards, and one to Brigadier General Cameron's brigade; two companies to the 4th division, being one for Major General Cole's, and one for Brigadier General A. Campbell's brigades; and three companies, with the Head-Quarters of the regiment, with the 3d division.

5. The Adjutant and Quarter-Master General will take measures

sures for placing under the orders of major General Picton an Officer belonging to each of their departments; and the Commissary General and Inspector of Hospitals, the same proportion of Commissariat and Medical Staff as attached to the other divisions of Infantry.

6. Captain Cockburne, Deputy Assistant Adjutant General, is attached to the 3d division of Infantry.

ADJUTANT GENERAL'S OFFICE.
G. O. *Vizeu, 23d February*, 1810.

CAPTAIN Dashwood, Deputy Assistant Adjutant General, is appointed to the 4th Division of Infantry vice Major Berkeley, Assistant Adjutant General, who is to return to Head Quarters.

ADJUTANT GENERAL'S OFFICE.
G. O. *Vizeu, 24th Feb.* 1810.

(Copy) HORSE GUARDS.
SIR, *26th Jan.* 1810.

1. HAVING had the honour to lay before the King the proceedings of a General Court Martial, held at Badajoz, on the 4th December, 1809, and continued by adjournment to the 8th of the same month, for the trial of Lieutenant Mathew Handcock, 45th Regiment, who was arraigned upon the under-mentioned charges:

FIRST CHARGE.

For absenting himself from his duty without leave whilst attached to the sick and wounded on the retreat of the General Hospital from Talavera, between the 3d of August and 14th October, 1809, and proceeding to Lisbon without

without authority, being prejudicial to good order and military discipline.

SECOND CHARGE.

For scandalous and infamous conduct, highly unbecoming the character of an Officer and a gentleman, in grossly insulting and threatening Captain Carthew, 39th Regiment, in a letter addressed to him, dated Campo Mayor, 14th October, 1809, whilst under an arrest for the preceding charge; the same being likewise prejudicial to good order and military discipline.

THIRD CHARGE.

For breaking his arrest by absenting himself from the Head-Quarters of his regiment on the 18th and 20th days of November, 1809, whilst under the said arrest, for the offence specified in the first charge.

Upon which charges the Court came to the following decision:

The Court having maturely and deliberately weighed and considered the evidence and information in support of the charges preferred against the prisoner, Lieutenant Mathew Handcock, 45th Regiment, as well as that which he has produced in his defence, are of opinion, that with respect to the first charge, that he the prisoner, Lieutenant Mathew Handcock, did quit a brigade of sick and go to Lisbon when on the retreat from Talavera; but it not appearing to the Court that the prisoner was duly informed of his being ordered for that duty, from the ill state of his health at the time, the general confusion which was prevalent, and his having mentioned his intention of going to Lisbon

Lisbon to Captain Lightfoot, the Court do acquit the prisoner, Lieutenant Mathew Handcock, of any improper conduct in having quitted the detachment and going to Lisbon.

The Court do find the prisoner guilty of the second charge, being in breach of the 28th article of the 16th Section of the Articles of War.

The Court do also find the prisoner guilty of the third charge, being in breach of the 27th article of the 16th Section of the Articles of War.

And do by virtue of the said articles sentence him the prisoner, Lieutenant Mathew Handcock, to be *cashiered.*

I have to acquaint your Lordship that his Majesty has been pleased to approve and confirm the finding and sentence of the Court.

Your Lordship will therefore acquaint me with the day upon which the sentence is made known to the prisoner, Lieutenant Mathew Handcock, as from that day he will cease to receive pay in his Majesty's service.

(Signed) D. DUNDAS.
Commander in Chief.

To Lieutenant General Lord
Visc. Wellington, &c. &c. &c.

2. Captain Wade, 42d Regiment, is appointed extra Aide-de-Camp to Major General the Honourable G. L. Cole.

G. O.

ADJUTANT GENERAL'S OFFICE.

G. O. *Vizeu, 26th Feb.* 1810.

SERJEANT Major Joshua Fothergill, of the Coldstream Guards, is appointed to act as Adjutant to the 88th Regiment till his Majesty's pleasure is known.

ADJUTANT GENERAL'S OFFICE.

G. O. *Vizeu, 27th Feb.* 1810.

THE following notifications of appointments and arrivals of Officers to join the Medical department have been received:

Surgeon William Vassal, from the 6th Foot, to be Surgeon to the Forces.

Acting Deputy Purveyor Harry Bacon to be Deputy Purveyor, vice Mapother, promoted.

Acting Deputy Purveyor John Winter to be Deputy Purveyor to the Forces.

The following Officers of the Medical Staff have arrived from England:

Hospital Mate John Davis . .	25th Jan. 1810.
——— S. W. Graves . .	
——— William Newton .	
——— Daniel M'Vea . .	
——— William Bassett .	
——— Morris Griffith .	
——— Charles Newcombe	
——— Henry Hart . .	
——— James Lowrey . .	
——— Henry Douglas .	
——— William Thompson	
——— Henry Develin . .	

Hospital

Hospital Mate Philip Luger . .
——— Charles M'Lean .
——— J. Bennet . . .
——— J. Dewey . . .
——— Thomas Prosser . } 31st Jan. 1810.
——— William Cartney .
——— Edward Graham .
——— W. Fisher . . .
——— Thomas Irwin . .

ADJUTANT GENERAL'S OFFICE.

G. O. *Vizeu, 28th Feb.* 1810.

1. AT a General Court Martial assembled by virtue of a warrant, and in pursuance of an order from his Excellency Lord Viscount Wellington, whereof Colonel the Honourable Edward Stopford was President, and Captain Goodman, Deputy Judge Advocate, held at Vizeu, the 22d February, 1810, was arraigned Privates Cornelius M'Guire, of the 3d battalion 27th Regiment, and George Chambers, 1st battalion 88th Regiment, for stopping on the high-way, and forcibly robbing, some Portuguese inhabitants, particularly Antonio Lopiz di Nis, whilst on the march from Tondella to Vizeu, on or about the 20th day of February, 1810; to which charges the prisoners pleaded not guilty.

OPINION AND SENTENCE.

The Court having maturely and deliberately weighed and considered the evidence adduced in support of the prosecution against the prisoners, Privates Cornelius M'Guire,

M'Guire, of the 3d battalion 27th Regiment, and George Chambers, 1st battalion 88th Regiment, together with what they have offered in their defence, are of opinion they are guilty of the charges preferred against them, being in breach of the Articles of War, and do by virtue thereof sentence them, the prisoners, Cornelius M'Guire, 3d battalion 27th Regiment, and George Chambers, 88th Regiment, to be *hanged by the neck till dead*, at such time and place as his Excellency the Commander of the Forces may deem fit; which sentence has been confirmed by his Excellency the Commander of the Forces.

2. The sentence of the General Court Martial on the trial of Cornelius M'Guire, of the 3d battalion 27th Regiment, is to be carried into execution on the afternoon of the 2d March, in presence of the troops stationed at Celorico, paraded for that purpose, under the direction of the Assistant Provost, 4th divisiou of Infantry.

3. The sentence of the General Court Martial on the trial of George Chambers, 1st battalion 88th Regiment, is to be carried into execution on the afternoon of the 3d March, in presence of the 88th Regiment, paraded for that purpose, and under the direction of the Provost Marshal of the army.

4. At a General Court Martial assembled by virtue of a warrant, and in pursuance of an order from his Excellency Lord Viscount Wellington, whereof Colonel the Honourable Edward Stopford was President, and Captain Goodman, Deputy Judge Advocate, held at Vizeu, the 23d day of February, 1810, was arraigned John M'Donough, private, 2d battalion 58th Regiment, for repeated desertions, particularly on or about the 29th day of December,

cember, 1809; to which charge the prisoner pleaded not guilty.

OPINION AND SENTENCE.

The Court having maturely and deliberately weighed and considered the evidence adduced in support of the prosecution against the prisoner, private John M'Donough, of the 2d battalion 58th Regiment, together with what he has offered in his defence, are of opinion he is guilty of the charge preferred against him, being in breach of the Articles of War, and do by virtue thereof sentence him, the prisoner, private John M'Donough, 2d battalion 58th Regiment, to be *shot to death*, at such time and place as his Excellency the Commander of the Forces may deem fit; which sentence has been confirmed by his Excellency the Commander of the Forces.

The sentence of the General Court Martial on the trial of John M'Donough, private of the 58th Regiment, is to be carried into execution, in presence of the troops, at Trancozo, paraded for that purpose, on the afternoon of the 3d of March, by a detachment of the 58th Regiment, under the direction of the Assistant Provost Marshal, 4th division, who will proceed to Trancozo on the morning of the 3d.

6. The Commander of the Forces draws the attention of the soldiers of the army to the consequence of the crimes committed by the soldiers thus ordered for execution under the sentence of a General Court Martial. Cornelius M'Guire, of the 27th Regiment, and George Chambers, of the 88th Regiment, committed a crime which the Commander of the Forces is concerned to ob-

serve

serve is too common in this army; they robbed and ill-treated an inhabitant of this country, whom they met on the road; a crime which the Commander of the Forces is determined in no instance to forgive.

The soldiers of the army have been invariably well treated by the inhabitants of Portugal; and the frequent instances which have occurred of their being robbed and ill treated, and of murders being committed, by soldiers who straggle from their detachments on a march, are a disgrace to the character of this army, and of the British nation.

The Commander of the Forces is therefore determined in every case of the kind that may occur to have proof adduced of the crime committed; and the sentences of the General Courts Martial, whatever they may be, shall be carried into execution.

The Commander of the Forces is concerned to observe that the crime committed by John M'Donough, private in the 58th Regiment, is no less common in this army than robbery and murder; and in respect to this crime he is equally determined to carry into execution the sentences of the General Courts Martial, whatever they may be.

7. Lieutenant Parry, 28th Regiment, and Lieutenant Fox, 66th Regiment, are to place themselves under the orders of Marshal Beresford.

ADJUTANT GENERAL'S OFFICE.

G. O. *Vizeu, 1st March,* 1810.

Memorandum.

Lieutenant Skeill,
Lieutenant M'Arthur, } 3d Regiment, or Buffs,

are to place themselves under the orders of Marshal Beresford.

ADJUTANT GENERAL'S OFFICE.

G. O. *Vizeu, 2d March,* 1810.

Memorandum.

Lieutenant Maxwell,
Lieutenant Creswell, } 74th Regiment,

are to place themselves under the orders of Marshal Beresford.

ADJUTANT GENERAL'S OFFICE.

G. O. *Vizeu, 3d March,* 1810.

1. THE several corps of the army will immediately transmit to the Quarter-Master General's Office returns for two hundred days bât, baggage, and forage money, for the period commencing the 1st instant and ending the 16th next September. Commanding Officers are referred to the printed Regulations respecting bât and forage allowance, dated May, 1809, and inserted in the General Orders, 1st September; as also to the Circular Letter of the

the Commander in Chief, dated Horse Guards, 17th July, 1809, and inserted in the General Orders, 23d September, 1809.

2. Captain Thorne, 3d Regiment, or Buffs, is appointed to act as a Deputy Assistant in the Quarter-Master General's department until his Majesty's pleasure is known.

ADJUTANT GENERAL'S OFFICE.
G. O. *Vizeu, 4th March*, 1810.

1. THE Commander of the Forces has great satisfaction in communicating to the General Officers, the Officers, Non-commissioned Officers, and soldiers of the army, who fought the Battle of Talavera, the following testimonies of the approbation of the Houses of Lords and Commons of their distinguished conduct:

(Copy)

MY LORD,

I HAVE the honour, by command of the Lords spiritual and temporal in parliament assembled, to enclose their resolution of thanks to your Lordship for the distinguished ability displayed by you on the 27th and 28th July last, in the glorious Battle of Talavera, which terminated in the signal defeat of the forces of the enemy, and to transmit at the same time the resolutions of their Lordships, respecting the distinguished exertions of the Officers, and the distinguished valour and discipline of the Non-commissioned Officers and Private Soldiers in that memorable battle.

I know not how, my Lord, to presume, when I am communicating these honourable sentiments, which the Illustrious House, in which these thanks have been voted to your Lordship, entertain of your Lordship's high merit, to express any feelings of the individual who has the honour to make this communication; but I cannot refrain from assuring your Lordship that I feel a satisfaction which I cannot adequately express, from the circumstance that I happen to be the instrument of addressing the thanks of the House to an Officer for his services in Spain, who has well earned and received the thanks and gratitude of his country for highly eminent services performed in so many parts of the dominions which belong to it.

(Signed) ELDON, C.

Die Veneris, 26*th Jan.* 1810.

Resolved, by the Lords spiritual and temporal in parliament assembled, that the thanks of this House be given to Lieutenant General Lord Viscount Wellington for the distinguished ability displayed by him on the 27th and 28th July last, in the glorious Battle of Talavera, which terminated in the signal defeat of the enemy's forces, and that the Lord Chancellor do communicate the same to him.

(Signed) GEORGE ROSE,
Clerk of Parliament.

Die Veneris, 26*th Jan.* 1810.

Resolved, Nemine Dissentiente, by the Lords spiritual and temporal in parliament assembled, that the thanks of this House be given to Lieutenant General Sir John Cope Sherbrooke,

Sherbrooke, Knight of the most Honourable Order of the Bath, to Lieutenant General William Payne, to Lieutenant General Sir Stapleton Cotton, Bart. to Lieutenant General Rowland Hill, to Major General Christopher Tilson, to Brigadier General Alexander Campbell, to Brigadier General Henry Frederick Campbell, to Brigadier General Richard Stuart, to Brigadier General the Honourable Charles Stewart, to Brigadier General Allan Cameron, to Brigadier General Henry Fane, to Brigadier General George Anson, and to Brigadier General Edward Howorth, and the several other Officers, for their distinguished exertions on the 27th and 28th July last, in the memorable Battle of Talavera, which terminated in the signal defeat of the forces of the enemy, and that Lieutenant General Lord Viscount Wellington do signify the same to them.

(Signed) GEORGE ROSE,
Clerk of Parliament.

Die Veneris, 26th Jan. 1810.

Resolved, Nemine Dissentiente, by the Lords spiritual and temporal in parliament assembled, that this House doth highly approve of and acknowledge the distinguished valour and discipline displayed by the Non-commissioned Officers and Private Soldiers of the Forces serving on the 27th and 28th July last, under the command of Lieutenant General Lord Viscount Wellington, in the glorious Victory obtained at Talavera, and that the same be signified to them by the Commanding Officers of the several corps, who are desired to thank them for their gallant and exemplary conduct.

(Signed) GEORGE ROSE,
Clerk of Parliament.

 3. (Copy)

3. (Copy) HOUSE OF COMMONS.
2d *Feb.* 1810.

MY LORD,

BY command of the House of Commons, I have the honour to communicate to your Lordship their thanks for the distinguished ability displayed by you on the 27th and 28th July last, in the glorious Battle of Talavera.

I am also to request that your Lordship will signify the thanks of the House to the several Officers serving under your command for their distinguished exertions upon those memorable days; and, in addition to these thanks, the House hath further declared its high approbation and acknowledgments of the distinguished valour and discipline displayed by the Non-commissioned Officers and Private Soldiers of the Forces then serving under your Lordship's command in that glorious Victory, which the Commanding Officers of the several corps are desired to signify to them, thanking them for their gallant and exemplary conduct. In presenting to your Lordship at the same time my own cordial congratulations upon the accession of honours which so justly accompanied such eminent services in the field, I must crave your pardon for expressing in any degree my personal sentiments of regret, that we must therefore necessarily lose the advantage of your parliamentary services in this House, where they were witnessed at all times with so much general satisfaction, and by no one with more sincere admiration than by myself.

(Signed) CHARLES ABBOTT.

To Lieut. General the Rt. Hon.
Lord Viscount Wellington,
&c. &c. &c.

Resolved,

Jovis 1° *die Feb.* 1810.

Resolved, That the thanks of this House be given to Lieutenant General Lord Viscount Wellington for the distinguished ability displayed by him on the 27th and 28th July last, in the glorious Battle of Talavera, which terminated in the signal defeat of the forces of the enemy.

Resolved, Nemine Contradicente,

That the thanks of this House be given to Lieutenant General Sir John Cope Sherbrooke, Knight of the most Honourable Order of the Bath, to Lieutenant General William Payne, to Lieutenant General Sir Stapleton Cotton, Bart. to Lieutenant General Rowland Hill, to Major General Christopher Tilson, to Brigadier General Alexander Campbell, to Brigadier General Henry Frederick Campbell, to Brigadier General Richard Stuart, to Brigadier General the Honourable Charles Stewart, to Brigadier General Allan Cameron, to Brigadier General Henry Fane, to Brigadier General George Anson, and to Brigadier General Edward Howorth, and the several other Officers, for their distinguished exertions on the 27th and 28th July last, in the memorable Battle of Talavera, which terminated in the signal defeat of the forces of the enemy.

Resolved, Nemine Contradicente,

That the House doth highly approve of and acknowledge the distinguished valour and discipline displayed by the Non-commissioned Officers and Private Soldiers of the Forces serving on the 27th and 28th July last, under the command of Lieutenant General Lord Viscount Wellington, in the glorious Victory obtained at Talavera, and that the same be signified to them by the Commanding Officers of the several corps, who are desired to thank them for their gallant and exemplary conduct.

Ordered,

That Mr. Speaker do communicate the said Resolutions to Lieutenant General Lord Viscount Wellington, and that he be requested by Mr. Speaker to signify the same to Lieutenant General Sir John Cope Sherbrooke, Knight of the most Honourable Order of the Bath, to Lieutenant General Payne, to Lieutenant General Hill, to Major General Tilson, to Brigadier General A. Campbell, to Brigadier General H. F. Campbell, to Brigadier General Stuart, to Brigadier General Cameron, and to Brigadier General Howorth.

(Signed) J. LEY.
Cl. D. Dom. Com.

4. Captain Burgh is appointed Aide-de-Camp to the Commander of the Forces, on the establishment, from the 24th February, 1810.

ADJUTANT GENERAL'S OFFICE.
G. O. *Vizeu, 6th March,* 1810.

THE General Court Martial, of which Colonel the Honourable Edward Stopford is President, is dissolved, and the members are to return to their duty.

ADJUTANT GENERAL'S OFFICE.
G. O. *Vizeu, 7th March,* 1810.

MR. J. L. Kemmington, and Mr. Charles Bonomie, are appointed Acting Assistant Commissaries until his Majesty's pleasure is known.

G. A. O.

ADJUTANT GENERAL'S OFFICE.

G. A. O. *Vizeu, 7th March*, 1810.

A GENERAL Court Martial will assemble at Vizeu, on Monday, the 12th March, 1810, at ten o'clock, for the trial of such prisoners as may be brought before it.

Brigadier General Alexander Campbell, President.

The members to be furnished by the 4th division of Infantry.

Names and dates of commissions of the members and list of evidences to be sent in, by the 10th instant, to the Adjutant General's Office, directed to the Deputy Judge Advocate; all evidences to be warned, and to attend.

ADJUTANT GENERAL'S OFFICE.

G. O. *Vizeu, 10th March*, 1810.

CAPTAIN Tripp, Deputy Assistant Adjutant General, is attached to the Cavalry; that Officer will proceed to Coimbra, and place himself under the orders of Lieutenant General Payne.

Captain Cotton, Deputy Assistant Adjutant General, will proceed to the Head-Quarters of the 2d division of Infantry, and place himself under the orders of Lieutenant General Hill.

ADJUTANT GENERAL'S OFFICE.

G. O. *Vizeu, 13th March,* 1810.

THE Paymasters of regiments, in the 3d, 4th, and light divisions of Infantry, and the Hussars, will repair to Head-Quarters for the purpose of receiving the balances still due on their estimates up to the 24th February, and also the amount of their respective estimates up to the 24th March.

ADJUTANT GENERAL'S OFFICE.

G. O. *Vizeu, 14th March,* 1810.

COLONEL Peacocke commanding at Lisbon, or any Officer commanding a station through which Lieutenant Glascott, 16th Light Dragoons shall pass, will put that Officer in arrest, and send him to Head-Quarters, for absenting himself from Abrantes without leave.

ADJUTANT GENERAL'S OFFICE.

G. A. O. *Vizeu, 14th March,* 1810.

CAPTAIN Green, 61st Regiment, is to proceed from Lisbon to Head-Quarters forthwith; Colonel Peacocke will see that he leaves Lisbon immediately after the receipt of this order.

ADJUTANT GENERAL'S OFFICE.
G. O. *Vizeu, 15th March,* 1810.

1. CAPTAIN Campbell, 74th Regiment, having expressed a desire to resign his situation upon the Staff, in order to join and do duty with his regiment, which has joined the army, the Commander of the Forces accepts his resignation, approves highly of his conduct in joining his regiment, and applauds the motives of it.

2. Serjeant Charles Smyth is appointed an Assistant Provost Marshal, and is to do duty with the 3d division of Infantry.

ADJUTANT GENERAL'S OFFICE.
G. O. *Vizeu, 16th March,* 1810.

LIEUTENANT Thomas Peacocke, 44th Regiment, is to place himself under the orders of Marshal Beresford.

ADJUTANT GENERAL'S OFFICE.
G. O. *Vizeu, 17th March,* 1810.

1. A BOARD, consisting of a Field Officer and two Captains of the 1st division, assisted by a Quarter-Master, to assemble to-morrow morning, at 11 o'clock, at the Commissary General's stores, to inspect and report upon the state of stores and provisions esteemed damaged.

2. Major Lindsay, 39th Regiment, is appointed Commandant of detachments, vice Brevet Major Murphy, 88th Regiment, resigned.

ADJUTANT GENERAL'S OFFICE.
G. O. *Vizèu, 18th March,* 1810.

1. THE Officers commanding regiments are, as soon as possible after the receipt of this order, to make a return, and report to the Quarter-Master General on the number and state of tents issued to the several regiments for the use of the Officers under the General Orders of the 24th May last.

2. Mr. Gunson, the Purveyor General, is forthwith to settle with the several regiments of the army for the stoppage received out of the pay of soldiers sent into the general hospitals, under the General Orders, 14th September.

After the 24th March, no advance of pay is to be sent with the soldiers to the general hospital; they are to be received into the general hospitals, under his Majesty's Regulations, 31st March, and 30th April, 1800, and the amount of the hospital stoppages to be settled according to his Majesty's Regulations of the 30th April, 1800.

ADJUTANT GENERAL'S OFFICE.
G. O. *21st March,* 1810.

THE Commander of the Forces refers the Officers commanding regiments to the orders they received through the Quarter-Master General, specifying the form in which the returns of the articles of field equipment were to be made, under the Orders of the 31st May, 1809.

He requests that the returns may hereafter be made out, according to that form, as specified underneath.

FORM

FORM

Of a Regimental Return of Articles of Field Equipment.

	Public Mules.	Tents.	Camp Kettles.	Bill-Hooks.	Canteens.	Haversacks.	Intrenching Tools.			
							Spades.	Shovels.	Pick-axes.	Felling-axes.
In possession . . .										
Wanting										

If any articles are returned wanting, a N. B. is to be made at the foot of the return, stating particularly the reason.

If any article should become unserviceable, a special report to be made on the subject.

Memorandum.—Regiments and corps will send in to the Adjutant General's Office, on or immediately after the 25th instant, a return of the Officers who may have been absent without leave during the preceding three months.

G. O.

ADJUTANT GENERAL'S OFFICE.

G. O. *Vizeu, 23d March,* 1810.

1. THE soldiers of the army are desired not to eat roots, particularly the onions which they find growing wild in the fields, and even in the gardens many of them are poisonous, and a Serjeant of the 57th Regiment has died of the consequences of eating some of them.

2. Hospital Mate Arthur Hamilton is appointed to act as Assistant Surgeon to the 2d battalion 39th Regiment, until his Majesty's pleasure is known.

3. Major Nixon, 2d battalion 28th Regiment, will place himself under the orders of Marshal Beresford.

ADJUTANT GENERAL'S OFFICE.

G. O. *Vizeu, 24th March,* 1810.

THE General Court Martial, of which Brigadier General Campbell is President, is adjourned to Celorico, where it will meet on Tuesday, at such hour as the President shall appoint.

ADJUTANT GENERAL'S OFFICE.

G. O. *Vizeu, 25th March,* 1810.

1. AT a General Court Martial assembled by virtue of a warrant, and in pursuance of an order from his Excellency Lord Viscount Wellington, whereof Brigadier General Campbell was President, and Captain Goodman, Deputy Judge Advocate, held at Vizeu, 21st March, 1810,

1810, were arraigned John Campbell, Cornelius Cowley, and John Cairney, privates in the 88th Regiment, upon the following charges:

FIRST CHARGE.

For having absented themselves from their quarters at Monforte after hours, on the night of the 7th and 17th December, 1809, having conspired to plunder the inhabitants in the neighbourhood of that town.

SECOND CHARGE.

For having in the course of the period above-mentioned plundered some Portuguese inhabitant or inhabitants, and for having attempted to enter into a house by force, whereby Private John M'Gowan, one of the party, was dangerously wounded.

THIRD CHARGE.

For deserting, on or about the 31st December, 1809, with arms and accoutrements whilst prisoners at Coimbra, for the crimes above charged.

FOURTH CHARGE.

For having resisted and fired upon the Magistrates and peasants authorized to retake them, on the 3d January, at the village of Espinhel, at the house of Emanual Peter Cazal.

OPINION AND SENTENCE.

The Court having maturely and deliberately weighed and considered the evidence adduced on the prosecution against the prisoners, Privates John Campbell, Cornelius Cowley,

Cowley, and John Cairney, 88th Regiment, together with what they have offered in their defence, are of opinion they are in part guilty of the first charge preferred against them, viz. Having absented themselves from their quarters, at Monforte, after hours, on some nights between the 7th and 17th December, 1809, and having conspired to plunder some inhabitant or inhabitants in the neighbourhood of that town.

The Court are further of opinion that the prisoners, Privates John Campbell and John Cairney, 88th Regiment, are guilty of the second charge preferred against them, viz. For having, in the course of the period abovementioned, plundered some Portuguese inhabitant or inhabitants, and for having attempted to enter into a house by force, whereby Private John M'Gowan, one of the party, was dangerously wounded; and that the prisoner Cornelius Cowley, 88th Regiment, is guilty of the first part of the second charge, viz. For having, in the course of the period above-mentioned, plundered some Portuguese inhabitant or inhabitants; but acquit him of the latter part of the second charge, viz. For having attempted to enter into a house, whereby Private John M'Gowan, one of the party, was dangerously wounded.

The Court are further of opinion that the prisoners are guilty of the third charge preferred against them, viz. For deserting, on or about the 31st December, with arms and accoutrements whilst prisoners at Coimbra, for the crimes above charged.

The Court are further of opinion that the prisoners, Privates John Campbell, Cornelius Cowley, and John Cairney, 88th Regiment, are guilty of the fourth charge preferred against them, viz. For having resisted and fired

upon

upon the Magistrates and peasants authorized to retake them, on the 3d January, at the village of St. Espinhel, and at the house of Emanuel Peter Cazal, being in breach of the Articles of War, and do by virtue thereof sentence them the prisoners, Privates John Campbell, Cornelius Cowley, and John Cairney, 88th Regiment, to be hanged by the neck till dead, at such time and place as his Excellency the Commander of the Forces may deem fit; which sentence has been confirmed by his Excellency the Commander of the Forces.

The sentence of the General Court Martial on John Campbell, Cornelius Cowley, and John Cairney, is to be carried into execution on Tuesday the 27th March, by the Assistant Provost attached to the 3d division, in presence of the troops, at Alverca, paraded for that purpose, under the command of the Commanding Officer at Alverca.

The Commander of the Forces requests that the Officers commanding regiments will draw the attention of the soldiers under their command to this example of the consequences of the disgraceful outrages of which too many of the soldiers of this army have been guilty.

The Commander of the Forces repeats his determination to spare no trouble to procure and produce evidence against those who may be guilty of such outrages, and to carry into execution invariably whatever may be the sentence of the Court Martial. His Excellency particularly requests the Commanding Officers of regiments to revert to the General Orders, and to draw the attention of the Officers and Non-commissioned Officers under their command to those orders which have for their object to prevent the commission of those crimes, and to render unnecessary these dreadful punishments, by the preservation of order and regularity among the soldiers, on their marches, in their quarters, and particularly on detachments.

3. The meeting of the General Court Martial, of which Brigadier General Campbell is President, at Celorico, is further adjourned till Wednesday.

4. The following appointments are to be considered in force until his Majesty's pleasure is known.

Hospital Mate Duncan Campbell to be Assistant Surgeon, 57th Regiment, vice Snow, deceased.

Hospital Mate David Wright to be Assistant Surgeon to the 2d battalion 48th Regiment, vice Maxwell, deceased.

Hospital Mate Samuel Holmes to be Assistant Surgeon to the 97th Regiment, vice Burke promoted to the 95th Regiment.

ADJUTANT GENERAL'S OFFICE.

G. O. *Vizeu, 27th March*, 1810.

1. WHEN green forage is issued, the ration is to consist of 28 lbs. and the quantity of corn as fixed by the General Order, 31st May, 1809.

The regiments in General Fane's brigade are to receive the quantity of corn as fixed by the General After Order, 31st January, 1810.

2. Captain Algeo, 2d battalion 34th Regiment, is to place himself under the orders of Marshal Beresford.

G. O.

ADJUTANT GENERAL'S OFFICE.
G. O. *Vizeu, 28th March,* 1810.

1. MR. Acting Assistant Commissary Purcell is appointed to the light division, and will relieve Mr. Assistant Commissary Drake, who, till further orders, is attached to Brigadier General Cameron's brigade.

2. The Paymasters of regiments in the 1st division, on application to the Deputy Paymaster General, this day or to-morrow, will receive a proportion of the amount due on their estimates up to 24th March.

ADJUTANT GENERAL'S OFFICE.
G. O. *Vizeu, 31st March,* 1810.

1. HIS Majesty has been pleased to appoint Colonel the Honourable Edward Pakenham to be Deputy Adjutant General to the Forces serving under his Excellency Lieutenant General Lord Wellington, bearing date 3d March, 1810.

2. The Commander of the Forces requests that the Officers of the army will not call for green forage as long as dry forage can be procured, unless it should be essentially necessary for their horses.

3. A General Court Martial will assemble at Coimbra on the 5th April, for the trial of such prisoners as may be brought before it.

Brigadier General Fane, President.

The Members to be furnished by the heavy brigade of Cavalry and troops stationed at Coimbra.

 Memo-

Memorandum.—Lieutenant Gregory, 29th Regiment, will place himself under the orders of Marshal Beresford.

ADJUTANT GENERAL'S OFFICE.

G. O. *Vizeu, 2d April,* 1810.

THE Officer commanding at Lisbon will order Captain Stainforth, 57th Regiment, to join his corps forthwith, and will see that he quits Lisbon for that purpose; he will fix the day on which Captain Stainforth is to reach the regiment, and he will communicate to the Officer commanding the 57th, the orders which he will have given to Captain Stainforth. Lieutenant Colonel Inglis will report to Head-Quarters Captain Stainforth's obedience to these orders, and that he has settled his accounts and paid the soldiers who came out under his command.

ADJUTANT GENERAL'S OFFICE.

G. O. *Vizeu, 3d April,* 1810.

Memorandum.—LIEUTENANT Dodwell, 23d Light Dragoons, will place himself under the orders of Marshal Beresford.

G. O.

ADJUTANT GENERAL'S OFFICE.

G. O. *Vizeu, 4th April,* 1810.

1. At a General Court Martial, assembled by virtue of a warrant, and in pursuance of an order from his Excellency Lord Viscount Wellington, whereof Brigadier General Campbell was President, and Captain Goodman Deputy Judge Advocate, held at Celorico, March 28th, 1810, were arraigned Alexander Sweeney, Patrick Brogan, and James Nugent, privates in the 3d battalion 27th Regiment, upon the following charge:

For burglariously entering the dwelling-house or shop of Joã Lopez Carriere, a Portuguese inhabitant, on or about the evening or night of the 21st February, 1810, at Celorico, and stealing thereout several articles of value.

To which charge the prisoners pleaded not guilty.

OPINION AND SENTENCE.

The Court having maturely and deliberately weighed and considered the evidence adduced in support of the prosecution against the prisoners, Privates Alexander Sweeny, Patrick Brogan, and James Nugent, 3d battalion 27th Regiment, together with what they have offered in their defence, and the evidence thereon, are of opinion that they are guilty of the charge preferred against them, viz. For burglariously entering the dwelling-house or shop of Joã Lopez Carriere, a Portuguese inhabitant, on or about the evening or night of the 21st February, 1810, at Celorico, and stealing thereout several articles of value, being in breach of the Articles of War, and do by virtue thereof sentence them, the prisoners, Privates Alexander Sweeny, Patrick Brogan, and James Nugent, to be hanged by by the neck till dead, at such time and place as his Excellency the Commander of the Forces may deem fit; which sentence has been confirmed by his Excellency the Commander of the Forces.

2. The sentence of the General Court Martial on the trial of Alexander Sweeny, Patrick Brogan, and James Nugent, privates, 3d battalion 27th Regiment, is to be carried into execution by the Assistant Provost attached to the 4th division of Infantry, in presence of the troops, at Guarda, paraded for that purpose, under the command of the Officer commanding at Guarda, on Friday, the 6th April, 1810.

The Commander of the Forces requests that the attention of the troops may be drawn to this additional example of the consequences of the bad conduct of the soldiers; the soldiers must see that it is impossible for them to commit these outrages without being discovered, and that conviction and punishment are the certain consequences of their crimes: indeed it has rarely happened that one of those who have conspired to commit these crimes, (for they are all the result of conspiracy,) has not offered himself as an evidence to convict the other criminals. The Commander of the Forces is obliged to observe that these crimes could not be so frequently committed, these conspiracies could not be formed, a robbery of the description of that for which these prisoners are now ordered for execution, could not have been known to the soldiers of almost the whole company, if the Non-commissioned Officers did their duty, and remained at all times among the soldiers.

His Excellency also observes that the Non-commissioned Officers can do their duty, and can maintain the authority

authority of their situation, only by having the support of the Officers belonging to their company given to them upon all occasions, by constant visiting the soldiers' quarters, and by invariable attendance upon the parade, from the moment the Soldiers are under arms. The Commander of the Forces draws the attention of the General and superior Officers of the army, and of all the other Officers, to his Orders of the 29th May, 1809, to which he desires a strict attention may be paid in future: it is impossible that the time of the Officers of the Army can be employed to so much advantage to the service, or with so much satisfaction to themselves, whilst the troops are in cantonments, as in giving their attention to support the authority of the Non-Commissioned Officers, to instil into them a just sense of their situation and of their duties, and thus to prevent these conspiracies and crimes, of which the Commander of the Forces finds himself under the necessity of making such frequent examples.

3. The General Court Martial of which Brigadier General Campbell is President is adjourned, and the Members are to return to their duty with their several Regiments.

Memorandum.—Captain Bermingham, 29th Regiment, and Lieutenant Salusberry, 62d Regiment, to place themselves under the orders of Marshal Beresford.

ADJUTANT GENERAL'S OFFICE.

G. O. *Vizeu, 5th April,* 1810.

THE Commander of the Forces calls the attention of the Officers of the Army to the General Orders 4th May,

Nos. 5 and 6, and of the 7th October, Nos. 8, 9, 10, and 11, also of the 8th Dec. No. 5; their inattention to these Orders is the greatest inconvenience to the service, increases the detail of business in the public Departments, renders necessary references to themselves and to the Commander of the Forces, on every article which they receive from the Magistrates of the country upon irregular vouchers: the whole of this might be avoided, if the Officers would attend to the Orders which have been issued upon this subject.

Irregular receipts and vouchers given by the following Officers are now before the Commander of the Forces.

Captain Boyce, 3d Guards, and Lieutenant Hill, 95th Regiment.

Assistant Surgeon O'Flaherty, 2d Bn. 5th Regiment.

Quarter Master Carter, Royal Waggon Train.

Captain Conolly, Quarter Master General's Department.

Lieutenant Freytag, 7th Line Bn. King's German Legion.

Quarter Master Fraser, 74th Regiment.

It will give the Commander of the Forces much concern to be under the necessity of requiring Officers who give irregular vouchers to the Magistrates of the country, to pay for the articles which they have received, but the frequent occurrence of inattention to these Orders which can be obeyed with so much facility, and the extent of the business which so much inattention throws upon all the Departments, will render this measure necessary.

G. A. O.

ADJUTANT GENERAL'S OFFICE.

G. A. O. *Vizeu, 6th April*, 1810.

THE Board, which has been sitting for the consideration of the claims of the Officers of the Army for losses, will be dissolved on the 12th instant.

ADJUTANT GENERAL'S OFFICE.

G. O. *Vizeu, 7th April*, 1810.

CAPTAIN CARROLL, 82d Regiment, is to place himself under the orders of Marshal Beresford.

ADJUTANT GENERAL'S OFFICE.

G. O. *Vizeu, 10th April*, 1810.

1. LIEUTENANT COLONEL ROOKE, 3d Regiment of Guards, is appointed to act as an Assistant Adjutant General until His Majesty's pleasure is known.

2. At a General Court Martial, assembled by virtue of a Warrant, and in pursuance of an Order from His Excellency Lord Viscount Wellington, whereof Brigadier General Henry Fane was President, and Major George Holmes, Acting Deputy Judge Advocate, held at Coimbra, 5th April, 1810, was arraigned Serjeant John Loar, 11th Regiment of Infantry, on the following charges.

1st *Charge*.—For plundering, or aiding and assisting in plundering, Emanuel Lete, a Portuguese inhabitant of Polerijo, near Pombal, on or about the 18th March, of a pair of boots, a dollar, and some vintains, while on the march

march and in command of an escort from Leiria to Coimbra.

2d Charge.—For having in possession the above stated boots, the property of Emanuel Lete a Portuguese, that were plundered.

Opinion and Sentence.—The Court having maturely weighed and considered the Evidence against the Prisoner, together with what he has offered in his defence, are of Opinion he is not guilty of the first Charge, and do therefore acquit him. On the second Charge, the Court are of Opinion the Prisoner, Serjeant John Loar, is guilty: viz. having in possession the above stated boots, the property of Emanuel Lete a Portuguese, that were plundered, being in breach of the Articles of War, and do therefore adjudge him to be reduced to the rank and pay of a private soldier. The Court are induced to award this lenient sentence, it appearing to them that the Serjeant, from severe indisposition or natural imbecility, was not aware of the impropriety of his conduct in purchasing those boots; which decision His Excellency the Commander of the Forces has been pleased to confirm.

The Court further proceeded to the trial of John Cruitz, Private, and Charles Anderson, Drummer, 5th Line Battalion, King's German Legion, arraigned on the following charges: viz. for entering the house of Bernardo Joseph de Feria, near Redinha, on their march from Leiria to Coimbra, on or about the 18th March, and taking therefrom the following articles: viz. a woman's cloak and petticoat, also a borico, the property of the said Bernardo Joseph de Feria, value about 17 dollars.

Opinion and Sentence.—The Court having maturely and deliberately considered the evidence against the prisoners,

soners, Private John Creutz and Charles Anderson, Drummer, 5th Line Battalion, King's German Legion, together with what they have offered in their defence, are of opinion as follows: viz. that Private John Creutz is not guilty of the crime laid to his charge, viz. for entering the house of Bernardo Joseph de Feria, near Redinha, on the march from Leiria to Coimbra, on or about the 18th March, 1810, and taking therefrom the following articles, viz. a woman's cloak and petticoat, as also a borico, the property of the said Bernardo Joseph de Feria, in value about 17 dollars, and do therefore acquit him of the same: That Drummer Charles Anderson upon the first part of the said charge, viz. for entering the house of Bernardo Joseph de Feria, near Redinha, on the march from Leiria to Coimbra, on or about the 18th March, 1810, and taking therefrom the following articles, viz. a woman's cloak and petticoat, is guilty, being in breach of the Articles of War; on the second part of the said charge, viz. as also a borico, the property of the said Bernardo Joseph de Feria, in value about 17 dollars, he is guilty of having the last in his possession, being in breach of the Articles of War, but not of taking it from the house of the said Bernardo Joseph de Feria; and do in consequence thereof sentence him the said Charles Anderson to receive 1000 lashes, at such time and place as His Excellency the Commander of the Forces shall direct, and to be put under stoppages not exceeding the half of his pay, till the sum of seventeen dollars is made good: which decisions severally have been confirmed by His Excellency the Commander of the Forces.

3. John Loar, 11th Regiment, and John Creutz, 5th

Line

Line Battalion, King's German Legion, are to be released from confinement.

Charles Anderson is to be sent prisoner to the 5th Line Battalion King's German Legion.

4. The General Court Martial of which Brigadier General Fane is President is dissolved, and the members are to return to their duty.

ADJUTANT GENERAL'S OFFICE.

G. O. *Vizeu*, 11*th April*, 1810.

1. WHENEVER articles of any description are supplied by the Commissary General to the troops, for which the troops are to pay, the Paymaster General must be furnished by the Commissary General with an account of the articles delivered to each Regiment, and their price if possible before the 24th of the month in which the articles will have been delivered, but at all events in the course of the succeeding month.

ADJUTANT GENERAL'S OFFICE.

G. A. O. *Vizeu*, 11*th April*, 1810.

A GENERAL Court Martial will assemble at Lisbon on the 17th instant for the trial of such prisoners as may be brought before it.

Major General Leith, President.

Members to be furnished by the Corps lately arrived at Lisbon: viz. 3d Bn. of the Royals, 1st Bn. 9th Regiment, and 2d Bn. 38th Regiment; names and dates of commissions, and list of evidences, to be sent into the Assistant Adjutant General's Office, addressed to the Deputy Judge Advocate on the 16th instant.

G. O.

ADJUTANT GENERAL'S OFFICE.

G. O. *Vizeu, 13th April,* 1810.

1. CAPTAIN WILLIAMS, 81st Foot, and Captain Brown, 60th Foot, will place themselves under the orders of Marshal Beresford.

2. Lieut. Colonel Rooke, Assistant Adjutant General, is attached to the 2d Division of Infantry, he will repair to Portalegre and place himself under the orders of Lieutenant General Hill.

G. A. O.—Head-Quarters will proceed tomorrow to Cea: all reports, &c. to be transmitted accordingly.

ADJUTANT GENERAL'S OFFICE.

G. O. *Cea, 14th April,* 1810.

HEAD-QUARTERS being established at Cea, the communication is in future to be carried on as follows:

The Parté established between Almeida and Cea will leave Almeida at 5 o'clock every morning, will leave Freixadas at ½ past 8, Celorico at ½ past 11, and will arrive at Cea at 5 in the afternoon.

The Letters from Almeida and the advanced posts, for Pinhel, are to be left at Freixadas, those for Guarda and Trancoso at Celorico, those for the rest of the army to come on to Cea.

The Officers commanding at Pinhel, Trancoso, and Guarda respectively will take care that their Letters for Head Quarters, or for other divisions of the army, or Lisbon, are with the Postmasters at the points of communication in time for the Parté.

The

The Parté will leave Head-Quarters every evening at 3 o'clock, will arrive at Celorico at 9 at night, at Freixadas at 1 in the morning, at Almeida at 5 in the morning. The Hussars are to remain upon the road between Celorico and Almeida, and the Guides between Celorico and Cea in case there should be occasion to communicate any intelligence besides the ordinary.

Communications by the Parté ———

A Guide will leave Cea every day at 12, will arrive at Mongualda at 5, at Vizeu at 8 in the evening.

A Guide will leave Vizeu every day at 12, will arrive at Mongualda at 3, and at Cea at 8 in the evening.

By this conveyance Letters are to be sent to Lieutenant General Sir John Sherbrooke's division of infantry and for the 16th Light Dragoons, to which they will be forwarded by the post from Vizeu to Tondella. The Parté for Thomar, Abrantes, Portalegre, Elvas and Badajos, will leave Cea every evening at 4 o'clock, and will arrive at Foz d'Avoure at 4 on the following morning, where he will leave letters for Coimbra, Lisbon, &c.

Memorandum.—Captain Gomersall, 2d Bn. 58th Regiment, and Lieutenant Waldron of the 5th Regiment, will place themselves under the orders of Marshal Beresford.

Ensign Phiffin, of the Buffs, may continue his services in the Portuguese Army.

ADJUTANT GENERAL'S OFFICE.

G. O. *Cea*, 17*th April*, 1810.

HEAD-QUARTERS will move to Vizeu tomorrow.

G. A. O.

ADJUTANT GENERAL'S OFFICE.

G. A. O. *Cea, 17th April*, 1810.

2. LIEUTENANT General Payne will transfer to the Royal Artillery such horses of the 3d Dragoon Guards, and 4th Dragoons, as may be cast from the Regiments, and may be deemed by the Officer of the Royal Artillery at Coimbra fit for that service; the others are to be made over to the Commissary at Coimbra, and such as are fit for the Waggon Train are to be retained in the service, and the others to be disposed of by public Auction.

ADJUTANT GENERAL'S OFFICE.

G. O. *Vizeu, 20th April*, 1810.

1. THE following General and Staff Officers have been appointed to the Staff of the army serving under Lieutenant General Lord Viscount Wellington, bearing date 12th January, 1810.

Major General Leith.

Lieutenant Hay, 29th Regiment, Aide-de-Camp.

Lieutenant Sir Godfrey Webster, 18th Hussars, extra Aide-de-Camp.

2. The following officers will place themselves under the orders of Marshal Beresford.

Lieutenant Appleton, ... 57th Regiment.
——— Dug. M'Gibbon, ... ditto.
——— Augustus M'Donald, . . . ditto.
——— Samuel Beresford Jermyn, . . ditto.
——— Holles, ... ditto.
——— Johnson, ... 40th ditto.

A. G. O.

ADJUTANT GENERAL'S OFFICE.

A. G. O. *Vizeu, 20th April,* 1810.

THE General Court Martial, ordered to assemble at Lisbon, in the orders of the 11th instant, is to consist of a President and 25 Members, to be furnished by the Regiments already named, and the 13th Regiment of Light Dragoons.

ADJUTANT GENERAL'S OFFICE.

G. O. *Vizeu, 21st April,* 1810.

1. THE communication with Head-Quarters is to be carried on as follows in future, instead of in the mode pointed out by the General Orders of the 15th instant.

The Parté for Head-Quarters will leave Almeida every morning at 7 o'clock, Fraxados ½ past 10, Celorico ½ past 2 in the morning, Mongualda 9 in the morning, and will arrive at Vizeu at 11 in the forenoon.

The Parté from Head-Quarters will leave Vizeu every afternoon at 4, will be at Mongualda at 6, at Celorico at 12, at Fraxados at ½ past 3 in the morning, and at Almeida at 7 in the morning.

The letters to and from Pinhel and Alverca are to be left at and taken up at Fraxados. Those to and from Guarda and Trancosa are to be left at and taken up from Celorico.

And the Officers commanding at the several stations will take care to have persons stationed to bring their letters to them from the places where they will be left.

2. The Hussars and Guides are still to remain stationed

upon

upon the road, notwithstanding that the Parté will pass daily.

3. The Parté for Thomar, Abrantes, Portalegre, Elvas, and Badajoz, will leave Vizeu at 4 o'clock every afternoon. He will leave at Santa Comba-daō letters for the 16th Light Dragoons, and at Foz d'Avoure those for Coimbra. He will take up at those places respectively the letters from them for Head-Quarters.

The communication between Head-Quarters and Lisbon will be carried on by the ordinary post.

ADJUTANT GENERAL'S OFFICE.

G. O. *Vizeu, 23d April,* 1810.

HIS Majesty has been pleased to appoint Captain Still, of the 3d or Buffs, to be a Deputy Assistant Quarter-Master General, bearing date January 15th, 1810.

ADJUTANT GENERAL'S OFFICE.

G. A .O. *24th April,* 1810.

THE Paymasters of the regiments in the 3d, 4th, and light divisions, the Paymaster of the 16th Light Dragoons, and of the regiments in General Fane's brigade, are to attend at Head-Quarters, and receive the balance of their estimates to the 24th April.

ADJUTANT GENERAL'S OFFICE.

G. O. *Vizeu, 25th April,* 1810.

1. CAPTAIN Meacham commanding the hospital at Coimbra is authorized to advance subsistence to the Officers on duty attached to the hospital, according to the mode pointed out in the following letter from the Paymaster General.

(Copy)

SIR, *Vizeu, 24th April,* 1810.

I BEG leave to submit for your consideration, as an accommodation to the service, that Captain Meacham should be empowered to issue to Officers, *upon their producing certificates from their respective Paymasters of the dates of which they have been paid,* a proportion of their monthly subsistence, taking their triplicate receipts for the same, which he may be directed to forward to me immediately, to enable me to deduct the amount at the first subsequent settling of the regimental estimates.

(Signed) J. P. BOYS.
Deputy Paymaster General.

To —— the Deputy Adjutant
General, &c. &c. &c.

2. Captain Cuthbert, of the Royal Fusileers, is appointed an extra Aide-de-Camp to Major General Picton.

3. The following Officers will place themselves under the orders of Marshal Beresford:

Brevet Major Austin, 58th Regiment.
Lieutenant Cullamore, 58th Regiment.
Lieutenant Queade, 40th Regiment.

G. O.

ADJUTANT GENERAL'S OFFICE.

G. O. *Vizeu, 26th April,* 1810.

LIEUTENANT General Sir John Sherbrook, K. B. having been under the necessity of quitting the army on account of the bad state of his health, Lieutenant General Sir Stapleton Cotton, Bart. is appointed to command the 1st division of Infantry.

ADJUTANT GENERAL'S OFFICE.

G. O. *Celorico, 29th April,* 1810.

1. THE Commander of the Forces refers the Officers commanding brigades and regiments to the Orders of the 24th May, 1809, Nos. 2 and 3, and those of the 21st March, 1810.

He is disposed to supply the Officers of the army with tents from the public stores, in the proportions and on the conditions specified in the General Orders above referred to; and it is requested that requisitions and returns may be made accordingly to the Quarter-Master General.

2. Whilst Head-Quarters shall be at Celorico, the Parté for Almeida will be dispatched every day at twelve at noon, will arrive at Fraxados at four, and at Almeida at eight in the evening.

The Parté for Coimbra, Thomar, and Elvas, will be dispatched every day at twelve at noon; this Parté will take letters for Lisbon. The Parté for Vizeu will set off every evening at four o'clock.

The Parté from Almeida for Head-Quarters, is to be dispatched as usual every evening at eight.

That from Vizeu for Head-Quarters every morning at eight o'clock.

3. The following Officers will place themselves under the orders of Marshal Beresford.

Captain Miller, 74th Regiment.
Lieutenant Hodges, } 61st Regiment.
Ensign Connor, }

4. Captain Cooke, Deputy Assistant Adjutant General, is attached to the 4th division of the Infantry, vice Captain Dashwood removed to the 1st division.

5. Serjeant Thomas Marshal, Coldstream Guards, is appointed Post-Master at Head-Quarters, bearing date 25th April.

ADJUTANT GENERAL'S OFFICE,
Celorico, 30th April, 1810.

G. O.

THE sick from the 3d, 4th, and light divisions are to be brought to Celorico on Thursday, instead of Trancoso on Wednesday, according to the former arrangement.

ADJUTANT GENERAL'S OFFICE.
Celorico, 1st May, 1810.

G. O.

1. CAPTAIN Lord James Hay, 4th West India Regiment, is appointed an Aide-de Camp to Lieutenant General Sir Stapleton Cotton, Bart. from the 25th April.

2. Mr. Assistant Commissary Ogilvie is appointed to act as a Deputy Commissary General, and is attached to the 2d division of Infantry from the 25th April.

ADJUTANT GENERAL'S OFFICE.
G. O. *Celorico, 4th May,* 1810.

1. THE frequent loss of money on its progress from one station to another, renders necessary the following regulations:

2. When any Officer of the Commissariat or Paymaster General's department takes charge of money to be transmitted from one station to another, they are to count it and place it in the different boxes or packages in which it is to be carried, and to see that those boxes or packages are well closed and secured.

3. When the money is to be removed, the Officer of the Commissariat or Pay department in charge is to see that all the boxes and packages are secured, and he will give them over in this state to the Officer or Non-commissioned Officer commanding the military escort; he will himself accompany the escort, and at the end of the march he will again inspect the boxes, have them all placed in his own Quarters, and apply for a sentry over the treasure.

4. The same practice must be repeated daily on the march till the arrival of the money to the place of its destination.

5. The money is to be counted and delivered over to the person to whom it had been consigned, in presence of the Officer of the Commissariat or Pay department in whose charge it had been sent; and he is to be responsible for all deficiencies from the hour from which he originally receives charge.

6. Whenever money is sent from one station to another, the Officer of the Commissariat or Pay department in charge must have with him a copy of these Orders.

 7. Major

7. Major Crookshanks, 38th Regiment, will place himself under the orders of Marshal Beresford.

ADJUTANT GENERAL'S OFFICE.

G. O. *Celorico, 7th May,* 1810.

1. THE sick of the 1st, 3d, 4th, and light divisions, will assemble at Celorico every Thursday fortnight, instead of weekly, as directed in the General Orders, 30th April; this arrangement to commence next Thursday week, till which time the sick will continue with their regiments.

2. The Commanding Officers of regiments are requested to send in accounts of the sums of money in their hands stopped from the soldiers for ammunition lost, &c.; these accounts to be made up to the 24th April.

3. Serjeant William Eggleton, 4th Dragoons, is appointed an Assistant Provost Marshal, vice Duval, deceased, from 25th April, 1810.

ADJUTANT GENERAL'S OFFICE.

G. A. O. *Celorico, 8th May,* 1810.

1. As it is necessary that Captain Humphrys should join the 3d battalion 27th Regiment, his appointment, as a Deputy Assistant in the department of the Quarter-Master General, is discontinued.

2. Brevet Major Marston, of the 48th Regiment, is appointed to act as an Assistant in the department of the Quarter-Master General till his Majesty's pleasure is known.

3. The

3. The General Officers commanding brigades, and Officers commanding regiments of Cavalry, are requested to adopt efficient measures to prevent the sale by the soldiers of the Cavalry of the grain intended for the horses; this object can be effected only by the constant attention of the Officers to their stable duties.

The Commander of the Forces likewise requests the Officers commanding brigades and regiments of Cavalry will communicate with the Magistrates in the several districts and villages in which the Cavalry are cantoned, to prevent the purchase by the inhabitants of the country of any article whatsoever from the soldiers, most particularly those destined for the food of the horses.

ADJUTANT GENERAL'S OFFICE.
G. O. *Celorico, 9th May,* 1810.

1. THE General Court Martial, of which Major General Leith is President, is adjourned till further orders, and the Members are to return to their duty with their several corps.

2. A General Court Martial, consisting of a President and fourteen Members, is to be assembled at Lisbon on Monday the 14th instant.

Colonel Saunders, 61st Regiment, President.

The Members to be furnished by the 83d, Royals, 9th, and 38th Regiments.

3. A General Court Martial is to assemble at Portalegre.

Brigadier General C. Craufurd, President.

The Members to be furnished by the 2d division of Infantry.

4. It is to be understood that Dragoons stationed upon the road between Head-Quarters and Lieutenant General Payne's quarters are not to be sent with letters, except by orders from Head-Quarters, or by Lieutenant General Payne; those between Guarda and Belmonte, except by orders from Major General Cole, or Major General Slade; nor those between Head-Quarters and the advanced posts, except by orders from Major General Picton, Brigadier General Crawford, or Brigadier General Cox, at Almeida.

5. The usual communication must be kept up by the Parté, which passes through or near all the quarters of the army, to and from Head-Quarters every day; and the Officers commanding at the different stations are requested to enquire and find out at what hours the Parté passes near their station, and to take care to have a person at the proper place on the high road to receive their letters, &c. and to deliver those intended for Head-Quarters.

ADJUTANT GENERAL'S OFFICE.

G. O. *Celorico, 12th May, 1810.*

MAJOR Ainsley, 4th Dragoons, is appointed to act as an Assistant in the Adjutant General's department until his Majesty's pleasure is known, and is attached to the Cavalry division.

G. O.

ADJUTANT GENERAL'S OFFICE.
G. O. *Celorico*, 13*th May*, 1810.

COLONEL De Grey, of the Royal Dragoons, is appointed a Colonel on the Staff, until his Majesty's pleasure is known, and is to join and take command of Brigadier General Fane's brigade of Cavalry, during the absence from it of Brigadier General Fane.

ADJUTANT GENERAL'S OFFICE.
G. A. O. *Celorico*, 14*th May*, 1810.

THE Officers of the Commissariat have been frequently urged to attend to the orders of the Commissary General; and the Commander of the Forces is concerned to have to observe that many of them have neglected to obey his orders in very important instances in which obedience was undoubtedly in their power.

He now publishes the names of Officers of the Commissariat from whom reports ought to have been received at stated periods of the state of the magazines and supplies in their charge, with the dates of the last reports received from each, shewing a neglect of an important duty, and a disobedience of a positive order.

The Commander of the Forces will take no further notice of this neglect, but to warn these gentlemen and others of the necessity of paying strict obedience to the orders of their superiors; and he assures them that the publication of their names to the army as persons guilty of disobedience and neglect will not be the only notice taken of such conduct in future.

***RETURN** of Commissariat Officers and Storekeepers in consequence of whose omission to transmit to the Commmissary General the periodical Returns of Supplies in their Charge, he is unable to furnish the Weekly Report to the Commander of the Forces.*

	Name of Officer, or Storekeeper.		Station, Brigade, or Corps.	Date of latest Report received.	Name of Officer superintending.
	Acting Assist. Comm.	Carey	Coimbra	April 26th.	Dep. Com. Gen. Lutyens
	Ditto	Kensington	Leiria	15th.	
	Mr. Schimitter		Cascaes	May 1st	Ditto Dunmore
	Mr. A. Cabral		Villa Nova	April 1st.	Ditto Boyes
	Mr. Kirton		Portalegre	24th.	Ditto Do.
	Act. Assist. Commis.	Belson	Major Gen. Tilson's	. . . .	during the Absence of
	Ditto	Wechinger	B. Gen. Stewart's	May 1st.	Acting Com. General
Commissary General's	Ditto	Wilkinson	——— C. Crauford	do.	Aylmer.
Office.	Ditto	Purcell	——— R. Crauford	April 8th.	Assist. Comm. Downie
Celorico, 14*th May*, 1810.	Ditto	Joly	Peniche	30th.	
	Mr. Petten		Agueda	29th.	
(Signed) J. Murray,	Assistant Commissary	Ragland	B. Gen. Cameron's	26th.	
Commissary General.	Acting Assist. Comm.	Strachan	Maj. Gen. Picton's	15th.	
	Ditto	Nelson	B. Gen. Campbell's	26th.	
	Ditto	Schauman	——— Fane	22d.	
	Ditto	Moore	Maj. Gen. Slade		
	Mr. Head		Reserve Artillery		

Adjutant General's Office.

G. O. *Celorico*, 16*th May*, 1810.

2. The Commander of the Forces desires that the Officers absent at Lisbon, on account of their health, will attend the Medical Boards when ordered; he now observes that Paymaster Knight, Captain Engel, and Quarter-Master Litchtewelden, did not attend a Medical Board when lately ordered.

3. Lieutenant George Fitzclarence, 10th Hussars, is appointed Aide-de-Camp to Brigadier General the Hon. Charles Stewart, vice Hoey, from the 25th ult.

4. Lieutenant Hoey, 18th Hussars, is attached as a Deputy Assistant to the Adjutant General's department, until His Majesty's pleasure is known.

5. Captain Baron Tripp, of the Adjutant General's department, is attached to the Cavalry, under the command of Brigadier General Fane, until further orders.

Adjutant General's Office.

G. O. *Celorico*, 17*th May*, 1810.

Captain Anderson, 42d Regiment, has permission to serve in the Portuguese army, and will report himself to Marshal Beresford.

G. O.

ADJUTANT GENERAL'S OFFICE.

G. O. *Celorico, 21st May,* 1810.

1. THE Officers commanding regiments of Infantry are requested to direct the Officers commanding companies, the Surgeons, and Paymasters, to prepare for the Commissary General bills for the allowance of one dollar per month for the shoeing of each mule employed in the carriage of camp kettles, Paymasters' books, and Surgeons' chests, since the 1st May, 1809.

2. The Officers commanding regiments of Cavalry will give the same directions to Officers commanding troops, Paymasters, and Surgeons.

3. These bills are to be made out for the whole regiment for each month, and must be countersigned by the Officer commanding the regiment, who must certify that the whole number of mules for which the allowance is demanded, have been kept for public service during the month.

4. The Quarter-Masters of regiments of Infantry, who have each a mule belonging to the public in his charge for the carriage of intrenching tools, are to send in their bills for the same allowance for the expence of shoeing this mule, to be countersigned and certified in the same manner by the commanding Officer of the regiment.

5. Similar bills are to be sent in by the regiments of Cavalry by those persons in charge, under the Orders of the 19th June, of the public mules attached to regiments of Cavalry, for the Veterinary Surgeon, Serjeant Armourer, Serjeant Sadler, and for the intrenching tools.

6. These bills are hereafter to be sent in at the end of every month.

7. The Commissary General will pay these bills, thus

signed

signed and certified, deducting from the amount of each those sums already paid on this account.

8. A General Court Martial will assemble at Pinhel on the 24th instant.

Colonel M'Kinnon, President.

The Members to be furnished by the 3d division of Infantry; Captain Andrews, 5th battalion 60th Regiment, will act as Deputy Judge Advocate.

ADJUTANT GENERAL'S OFFICE.

G. O. *Celorico, 22d May,* 1810.

Memorandum.—THE following Regiments have omitted to send in returns of sums stopped for ammunition lost by neglect, called for by the Orders, 7th May, viz.

1st or Royal Dragoons.	38th Foot.
13th Light Dragoons.	40th ditto.
14th ditto.	43d ditto.
16th ditto.	83d ditto.
1st ditto, K. G. L.	95th ditto.
5th Foot, 2d battalion.	97th ditto.
Royal Fusileers, 2d ditto.	1st Light Bat. K. G. L.
11th Foot.	2d ditto, ditto.
27th ditto.	Royal Staff Corps.

ADJUTANT GENERAL'S OFFICE.

G. O. *Celorico, 28th May,* 1810.

1. MAJOR Campbell, 74th Regiment, to place himself under the orders of Marshal Beresford.

2. Pay-

2. Paymasters of regiments of the 3d, 4th, and light divisions, and of the Cavalry, are to come to Head-Quarters to receive money on account of their estimates to the 24th of May.

ADJUTANT GENERAL'S OFFICE.
G. O. *Celorico, 29th May*, 1810.

(Copy.) HORSE GUARDS,
23d *April*, 1810.

MY LORD,

1. HAVING had the honour to lay before the King the proceedings of a General Court Martial, held at Vizeu, on the 12th March, 1810, and continued by adjournment till the 14th of the same month, for the trial of Lieutenant Alexander Winckstern, 7th line battalion King's German Legion, who was arraigned upon the under mentioned charges, viz.

FIRST CHARGE.

For highly unofficerlike conduct in having absented himself from his regiment, from or about the month of December, 1808, to the month of April, 1809, or thereabouts, under the pretext of sickness, without forwarding the necessary certificates of his indisposition, until repeatedly written to by his Commanding Officer to state the reason of his absence.

SECOND CHARGE.

For highly unofficerlike conduct in having absented himself from his regiment, from or about the 3d June, 1809,

1809, to the 26th October, 1809, or thereabouts, during which period his regiment was employed in actual service in Spain, under pretext of sickness, and neglecting to send in the medical certificates of his indisposition, or to give any satisfactory reason for his absence to his Commanding Officer, and not returning to his regiment or the army till brought back in custody of an Assistant Provost Marshal.

THIRD CHARGE.

For disobedience of orders in the month of September, 1809, or thereabouts, by not joining his battalion when ordered so to do, by Major Bergher, his Commanding Officer.

Upon which charges the Court came to the following decision:

The Court having maturely and deliberately weighed and considered the evidence adduced in support of the prosecution against the prisoner, Lieutenant Alexander Winckstern, 7th line battalion King's German Legion, together with what he has brought forward in his defence, and the evidences thereon, are of opinion he is guilty in part of the first part of the first charge preferred against him, viz. For highly unofficerlike conduct in having absented himself from his regiment, from or about the 6th day of February, 1809, to the 14th of the same month, and from or about the 28th day of February, 1809, to the 26th April, or thereabouts, under pretext of sickness; and that he is guilty of the latter part of the first charge, viz. Not forwarding the necessary certificates of his indisposition, until repeatedly written to by his Commanding Officer to state the reason of his absence.

The

The Court are further of opinion that the prisoner, Lieutenant Alexander Winckstern, 7th line battalion King's German Legion, is guilty of the second and third charges preferred against him, being in breach of the Articles of War, and do by virtue thereof sentence him, the prisoner, Lieutenant Alexander Winckstern, 7th line battalion King's German Legion, to be cashiered.

I am to acquaint your Lordship that his Majesty was pleased to approve and confirm the finding and sentence of the Court.

Your Lordship will therefore acquaint me with the day upon which the sentence is made known to the prisoner, Lieutenant Alexander Winckstern, as from that day he will cease to receive pay in his Majesty's service.

(Signed) D. DUNDAS.
Commander in Chief.

To Lieutenant General Rt. Hon. Visc. Wellington, K. B. commanding the British Troops in Portugal.

2. At a General Court Martial, assembled by virtue of a warrant and in pursuance of an order from his Excellency Viscount Wellington, whereof Brigadier General C. Craufurd was President, and Captain Conway Benning, Acting Deputy Judge Advocate, held at Portalegre, 22d May, 1810, was arraigned Lieutenant William Davy, 2d battalion 66th Regiment, on the following charge, viz.

For accepting a challenge, and fighting a duel, with the late Lieutenant John Lister, 2d battalion 66th Regiment, in in which duel the said Lieutenant John Lister was killed, on the 19th April, 1810, near Portalegre.

OPINION AND SENTENCE.

The Court having maturely considered the evidence in support of the prosecution brought forward by Lieutenant Colonel Colburne, are of opinion that the charge alleged against the prisoner, Lieutenant William Davy, is not proved, and do therefore acquit him; which decision has been confirmed by his Excellency the Commander of the Forces.

3. At a General Court Martial assembled by virtue of a warrant and in pursuance of an order from his Excellency Lord Viscount Wellington, whereof Brigadier General C. Craufurd was President, and Captain C. Benning, 66th Regiment, Acting Deputy Judge Advocate, held at Portalegre, 23d May, 1810, was arraigned Lieutenant Lambrecht and Ensign Witney 2d battalion 66th Regiment, on the following charge, viz.

For being seconds in a duel fought by Lieutenant William Davy and Lieutenant John Lister, in which duel the said Lieutenant John Lister was killed, on the 19th April, 1810, near Portalegre.

OPINION AND SENTENCE.

The Court having maturely considered the evidences brought forward in support of the prosecution by Lieutenant Colonel Colburne, are of opinion that the charge alleged against the prisoners, Lieutenant Lambrecht and Ensign Witney, is not proved, and do therefore acquit them; which decision His Excellency the Commander of the Forces has been pleased to confirm.

4. At a General Court Martial, assembled by virtue of a warrant and in pursuance of an order from his Excellency Lord Viscount Wellington, whereof Colonel M'Kinnon, 2d Foot Guards, was President, and Captain Andrews, 5th battalion 60th Regiment, Acting Deputy Judge Advocate, held at Pinhel, 24th May, 1810, was arraigned John Egan, private in the 88th Regiment, on the following charge, viz.

For deserting from his regiment, on or about the 18th May, 1810.

OPINION AND SENTENCE.

The Court having maturely and deliberately considered the evidence on the part of the prosecution, as well as the defence of the prisoner, are of opinion that the said John Egan, private soldier in the 88th Regiment of Foot, is guilty of the crime alleged against him, viz. For deserting from his regiment, on or about the 18th May, 1810, being in breach of the Articles of War; and do therefore sentence him, the said John Egan, private soldier in the 88th Regiment, to be transported as a felon for the term of seven years, and at the expiration of seven years to be at the disposal of His Majesty, to serve as a soldier in any of His Majesty's forces at home or abroad, for life; which sentence his Excellency the Commander of the Forces has been pleased to confirm.

5. At a General Court Martial assembled by virtue of a warrant and in pursuance of an order from his Excellency Lord Viscount Wellington, whereof Colonel M'Kinnon, 2d Foot Guards, was President, and Captain Andrews, 5th battalion 60th Regiment, Acting Deputy Judge Advocate, held at Pinhel, 26th May, 1810, was arraigned

arraigned William Seward and Bartholomew Kilbright, both privates in the 1st battalion 88th Regiment, on the following charge, viz.

For deserting from their regiment, on or about the 18th May, 1810.

OPINION AND SENTENCE.

The Court having most maturely weighed and considered the evidences on the part of the prosecution, as well as the defence of the prisoner, Private William Seward, 1st battalion 88th Regiment, are of opinion that he is guilty of the crime laid to his charge, viz. For deserting from his regiment, on or about the 18th May, 1810, being in breach of the Articles of War, and do therefore sentence him, the prisoner William Seward, private soldier in the 1st battalion 88th Regiment, to suffer death by being shot, at such time and place as his Excellency the Commander of the Forces shall deem fit.

The Court next proceeded to deliberate on the evidence adduced in support of the prosecution, as well as the defence of the prisoner Bartholomew Kilbright, private in the 1st battalion 88th Regiment, and are of opinion that he is guilty of the crime alleged against him, viz. For deserting from his regiment, on or about the 18th May, 1810, being in breach of the Articles of War, and do therefore sentence him, the said Bartholomew Kilbright, private soldier in the 1st battalion 88th Regiment, to receive 800 lashes on the bare back with a cat-o'-nine-tails, at such time and place as his Excellency the Commander of the Forces shall think fit.

The Court cannot conclude its proceedings without remarking that it has been induced to pass the above lenient sentence on the prisoner, Private Bartholomew Kilbright, in consequence of this being the first offence of any kind that he appears ever to have been guilty of, and also in consequence of the very excellent character given of him by his Commanding Officer and other Officers of the regiment.

The above decision has been confirmed by his Excellency the Commander of the Forces.

6. The sentence of the General Court Martial on the trial of William Seward and Bartholomew Kilbright, privates in the 88th Regiment, is to be carried into execution in the presence of the troops cantoned at Pinhel, to be paraded for that purpose, on the evening of the 1st of June.

That on the prisoner Seward by a Serjeant's party, 88th Regiment, under the direction of the Assistant Provost of the 3d division.

That on Private Kilbright by the Drummers of the 88th Regiment, under the direction of the same Officer.

The Commander of the Forces trusts that this awful example will deter others from the crime of desertion to the enemy, of which those soldiers have been guilty.

John Egan is to be put in irons, and sent to the Provost at Head Quarters.

7. The Officers in charge of the hospital at Coimbra will put Mr. William Collins, a Clerk in the Commissariat, in arrest, and send him to Head Quarters, in charge of the Assistant Provost at Figuera; Mr. Collins will be found at Figuera, or Coimbra.

The Assistant Provost at Figuera will be relieved at Cea, by the Assistant Provost attached to the Cavalry.

G. A. O.

ADJUTANT GENERAL'S OFFICE.

G. A. O. *Celorico, 31st May,* 1810.

THE 1st division of Infantry, the 16th Light Dragoons, the heavy brigade of Cavalry and the reserve Artillery, will be in readiness to march in the morning; routes will be sent to them this evening, or in the night, if the march should be necessary.

ADJUTANT GENERAL'S OFFICE.

G. O. *Celorico, 1st June,* 1810.

(Copy) HORSE GUARDS,

MY LORD, *3d May,* 1810.

1. HAVING had the honour to lay before the King the proceedings of a General Court Martial, held at Vizeu, on the 20th March, 1810, for the trial of Thomas Richardson, late Clerk in the Commissariat department, who was arraigned upon the under-mentioned charge, viz.

For scandalous and infamous conduct in misapplying and embezzling the public monies, by fraudulently receiving 5*l.* per cent. out of payments made by him at different times, about the months of September and October, 1809, at Merida.

Upon which charge the Court came to the following decision:

The Court having maturely and deliberately weighed and considered the evidence adduced in support of the prosecution against the prisoner, Thomas Richardson, late Clerk in the Commissariat Department, together with what he has offered in his defence, and the evidence thereon,

thereon, are of opinion that he is guilty of the charge preferred against him, being in breach of the Articles of War, and do by virtue thereof sentence him, the prisoner Thomas Richardson, late Clerk in the Commissariat Department, to three months imprisonment from the day of the date of the confirmation of this Court Martial, and also to refund the sum of 161*l.* 18*s.* 6*d.* being the amount received by him, in a fraudulent manner, out of the payment made to Manoel Fernandes, and Fernando de Tono, at Merida, on 3238*l.* 14*s.* 1*d.*; and in default of payment of the said sum of 161*l.* 18*s.* 6*d.* the Court do sentence the prisoner, Thomas Richardson, late Clerk in the Commissariat Department, to be committed to prison for six calendar months, there to remain, without bail, and until he shall pay such deficiency; and the Court do further adjudge him, the prisoner Thomas Richardson, late Clerk in the Commissariat Department, to be incapable and unworthy of again serving His Majesty in any situation of trust, either civil or military.

I am to acquaint your Lordship that His Majesty was pleased to approve and confirm so much of the finding and sentence of the Court as adjudges the prisoner to three months imprisonment, from the day of the date of the confirmation of this Court Martial, and to be incapable and unworthy of again serving His Majesty in any situation of trust, civil or military; and to remit the remainder of the sentence.

(Signed) DAVID DUNDAS,
Commander in Chief.

To Lieut, General Vis. Wellington, commanding the British Troops in Portugal.

3. The

3. The Commander of the Forces republishes an order given out by the late Commander of the Forces; and it is to be understood that the stoppage from the soldier, on account of cartridges lost or made away with, ought always to have been, and must in future be, 4*d*. for each cartridge, and 1*d*. for each flint.

It is not intended, however, to open again old accounts for those losses.

ADJUTANT GENERAL'S OFFICE.

A. G. O.

Celorico, 2d June, 1810.

1. THE Officers commanding regiments of Infantry are requested, as soon as possible, to make the following arrangement for sending into store the great coats or the blankets belonging to the regiments under their command respectively, according to the returns they before made upon this subject.

2. The blankets to be sent in are to be made up in bales, each containing fifty blankets; and if the bales which brought the blankets to the army, should be lost or mislaid, a blanket may be used as the bale to hold the others.

3. The great coats must each be marked with the name of the soldier to which it belongs, and his company and his regiment. The great coats must likewise be made up into bales, each containing fifty great coats; and each bale must be marked, viz. Great Coats belonging to ——— Regiment.

4. Application must be made to the Commissary of the brigade or division to convey the great coats or blankets

 belonging

belonging to regiments in the 1st, 3d, and 4th divisions, to Celorico, where they will be lodged in store.

5. Those belonging to regiments in the light division will be sent to Almeida.

Those belonging to regiments in the 2d division will be sent to Abrantes; and those to regiments in Lisbon to be lodged in store at Lisbon.

6. The Officers commanding regiments are to send in a report to the Quarter-Master General, specifying what number of blankets or great coats each has sent into store.

ADJUTANT GENERAL'S OFFICE.

A. G. O. *Celorico, 2d June,* 1810.

THE blankets and great coats must be made up in bales, each containing 25 blankets, or great coats, instead of 50, as ordered in the Orders of this morning.

ADJUTANT GENERAL'S OFFICE.

G. O. *Celorico, 3d June,* 1810.

1. LIEUTENANT General Sir S. Cotton is to take the command of the Cavalry.

2. Lieutenant General Sir B. Spencer has been appointed by his Majesty second in command to the Forces serving in Portugal, and will take the command of the 1st division of Infantry.

Memorandum.—List of deaths which took place on the removal

removal of the sick from Elvas to Lisbon, has been furnished to the Adjutant General in the manner hereafter stated; by neglect at the time, the names of the individuals were not taken, but only the numbers of each regiment. It is therefore very desirable that Officers commanding regiments should make every possible inquiry from Officers who may have been in charge of the sick at the same period, and ascertain, and report in writing to the Adjutant General's Department, the names of men who are stated to have died.

ADJUTANT GENERAL'S OFFICE.

G. O. *Celorico, 4th June,* 1810.

1. AT a General Court Martial, held by virtue of a warrant and in pursuance of an order from his Excellency Lord Viscount Wellington, of which Brigadier General C. Craufurd was President, and Captain C. Benning, 2d battalion 66th Regiment, Acting Deputy Judge Advocate, held at Portalegre, 30th May, 1810, was arraigned Richard Charlton and Thomas Barrow, privates of the 1st battalion 48th Regiment, on the following charges:

1st, For quitting their quarters, on or about the night of the 5th instant.

2d, Forcing into the house of De Cano, an inhabitant of the country, near Portalegre, and ill-treating the inhabitants, and plundering them of clothes and property, on the night of the 5th instant.

3d, Murdering De Cano, on the night of the 5th inst.

OPINION

OPINION AND SENTENCE.

The Court having maturely weighed and considered the evidence against the prisoners, Richard Charlton and Thomas Barrow, and what they have alleged in their defence, do find them guilty of the entire charges brought against them, being in breach of the Articles of War, and do therefore sentence each of them, Richard Charlton and Thomas Barrow, to be hanged by the neck until dead, at such time and place as his Excellency the Commander of the Forces may think proper; which sentence his Excellency the Commander of the Forces has been pleased to confirm.

2. The sentence of the General Court Martial on the trial of Richard Charlton and Thomas Barrow, of the 1st battalion 48th Regiment, is to be carried into execution at the Head-Quarters of Lieutenant General Hill's division, on Saturday, the 9th instant, under the direction of the Assistant Provost attached to the 2d division of Infantry, in presence of the troops at the same station, to be paraded for that purpose.

3. The Commander of the Forces is concerned to be obliged to bring before the troops another example of the consequence of their irregularities, breach of discipline, and crimes.

In order to get liquor, these soldiers formed a conspiracy to commit a robbery; in the course of the commission of this crime, one of a greater enormity, a murder, is committed, which is soon discovered. Then the parties to the commission of these crimes are eager to give information against each other, and the result is an exam-

ple,

ple, such as that which will be brought before the troops upon this occasion.

If such frequent instances had not occurred of the same circumstances produced by the same unvaried course of events, it would not be credible that British soldiers should so far forget their duty as to conspire to commit a robbery on a people they are sent to protect, and by whom they have been invariably well treated, and should murder in cool blood a fellow creature who had done them no injury, more particularly having a knowledge that those guilty of these crimes are invariably discovered, that the conspirators invariably inform against each other, and that the result of the trial must be the execution of the criminals.

The Commander of the Forces repeats his determination to persevere in carrying into execution the sentence of every General Court Martial on crimes of this description, in the fervent hope that each of them, which he will confirm, will be the last which he will have to consider.

4. Captain Preston and Captain Brown, 40th Regiment, are appointed Aides de Camp to Lieutenant General Sir B. Spencer.

Captain Drake, 95th Regiment, is appointed an extra Aide de Camp to Lieutenant General Sir B. Spencer, by permission of the Commander in Chief.

Captain Lawrie, 79th Regiment, is appointed Aide de Camp to Brigadier General Cameron, from the 15th April.

G. O.

ADJUTANT GENERAL'S OFFICE,

G. O. Celorico, 6th June, 1810.

THE General Court Martial, of which Major General Leith is President, is to assemble at Lisbon, at such time and place as the Major General shall appoint, with the exception of Major Crookshank, 38th Regiment, and those Members of the General Court Martial who are Officers of the 18th Light Dragoons, who are excused the further attendance on this Court Martial.

ADJUTANT GENERAL'S OFFICE,

G. O. Celorico, 7th June, 1810.

1. AT a Brigade Court Martial, held in pursuance of an order from Colonel the Honourable Edward Stopford, Celorico, 6th June, 1810, whereof Lieutenant Colonel Guise, 3d Guards, was President, was arraigned Serjeant Hall, 74th Regiment, confined by order of the Adjutant General, for being drunk on duty, the 4th June, 1810, whilst escorting a party of deserters from the enemy, who were placed in his charge to Celorico:

The Court having duly considered the evidence for and against the prisoner, do find him guilty of being in liquor, but not so much so as to render him incapable of doing his duty, and therefore sentence him to be suspended from rank and pay as a Serjeant for three calendar months; which sentence has been confirmed by his Excellency the Commander of the Forces.

2. The Commander of the Forces publishes this sentence to the army in order to shew his determination to bring to trial

trial those Non-commissioned Officers who disgrace themselves, and prove that they are not fit for their situations.

3. At a General Court Martial held by virtue of a warwant and in pursuance of an order from his Excellency Lord Viscount Wellington, held at Pinhel, 4th June, 1810, whereof Colonel M'Kinnon, 2d Foot Guards, was President, and Captain Andrews, 5th battalion 60th Regiment, Acting Deputy Judge Advocate, was arraigned Drummer Francetz, of the 7th line battalion King's German Legion on the following charge, viz.

For discharging his piece, and wilfully murdering his comrade, Drummer Barbant, of the same battalion, on or about the 26th May, 1810.

OPINION AND SENTENCE.

The Court having most maturely deliberated upon the whole of the evidence adduced on the part of the prosecution, as well as the defence of the prisoner, is of opinion that the prisoner, Drummer Francetz, 7th line battalion King's German Legion, is guilty of the crime laid to his charge, viz. For discharging his piece, and wilfully murdering his comrade, Drummer Brabant, of the same battalion, on or about the 26th May, 1810, being in breach of the Articles of War, and do therefore sentence him, the said Drummer Francetz, 7th line battalion King's German Legion, to be hanged by the neck till dead, at such time and place as his Excellency the Commander of the Forces shall think fit; which sentence has been confirmed by his Excellency the Commander of the Forces.

4. The sentence of the General Court Martial on the trial of Drummer Francetz is to be carried into execution, at the Quarters of the German Legion, on the evening of the

the 9th instant under the direction of the Assistant Provost attached to Sir B. Spencer's division, in presence of the troops at that station, to be paraded for this purpose.

5. A General Court Martial held by virtue of a warrant and in pursuance of an order from his Excellency Lord Viscount Wellington, held at Pinhel, 4th June, 1810, whereof Colonel M'Kinnon, 2d Foot Guards, was President, and Captain Andrews, 5th battalion 60th Regiment, Acting Deputy Judge Advocate, Michael Fahie, private in the 45th Regiment, was arraigned on the following charge, viz.

For deserting from his regiment, on the march from Villa de Rey to Pinhel, at Portalegre, on or about the 19th December, 1809.

OPINION AND SENTENCE.

The Court, having maturely and deliberately considered the evidence brought forward on the part of the prosecution, as well as the defence of the prisoner, is of opinion that the prisoner, Michael Fahie, private soldier in the 45th Regiment, is guilty of the crime alleged against him, viz. For deserting from his regiment, on the march from Villa de Rey to Pinhel, at Portalegre, on or about the 19th December, 1809, being in breach of the Articles of War, and do therefore sentence him, the said Michael Fahie, private soldier in the 45th Regiment, to be transported as a felon for the term of seven years, and at the expiration of the said term of seven years, to be at the disposal of His Majesty, to serve as a soldier in any of His Majesty's forces, at home or abroad, for life; which sentence has been confirmed by his Excellency the Commander of the Forces.

6. Michael

6. Michael Fahie, 45th Regiment, is to be sent to the Provost at Head Quarters, under a guard.

ADJUTANT GENERAL'S OFFICE.

A. G. O. *Celorico, 7th June,* 1810.

THE Paymasters of the under-mentioned regiments will repair forthwith to Almeida, where an Officer of the Paymaster General's Department will be on the 9th instant, to pay the money on account of their estimates.

Regiments { 3d Division.
Light Division.
Hussars King's German Legion.

ADJUTANT GENERAL'S OFFICE.

G. O. *Celorico, 8th June,* 1810.

1. COMMISSARY GENERAL Kennedy will take charge of the Commissariat Department, on Monday, the 11th inst.

2. As forage corn becomes very scarce, the Commissary General has been directed to issue 2lb. of dry, or 4lb. of green forage, for every pound of corn he may be under the necessity of issuing short of the allowed ration.

ADJUTANT GENERAL'S OFFICE.

G. O. *Celorico, 9th June,* 1810.

Memorandum.—THE Paymasters of the heavy brigade of Cavalry, 16th Light Dragoons, 1st and 4th

divisions

divisions of Infantry, are forthwith to attend at Head Quarters to receive a proportion of money, on account of their estimates, due to the 24th May.

ADJUTANT GENERAL'S OFFICE.

G. O. Celorico, 15th June, 1810.

CAPTAIN Pelly, 16th Light Dragoons, is appointed Aide de Camp to Brigadier General Anson.

ADJUTANT GENERAL'S OFFICE.

G. O. Celorico, 16th June, 1810.

1. ACCORDING to recent instructions which the Commissary General has received, it appears that single returns and receipts for rations alone are required, of which the army will take notice.

2. Mr. Acting Deputy Commissary Filder is attached to the 3d Dragoon Guards.

3. Lieutenant Owens, 16th Light Dragoons, is to put himself under the orders of Marshal Beresford.

4. Captain Sinclair, 1st Foot or Royals, is to put himself under the orders of Marshal Beresford.

ADJUTANT GENERAL'S OFFICE.

G. O. Celorico, 20th June, 1810.

1. MAJOR Macgregor Murray, 103d Regiment, is appointed to act as an Assistant Adjutant General, until His Majesty's

Majesty's pleasure is known, and to do duty with the troops stationed at Cadiz.

2. The Officers commanding regiments are requested to direct that the money stopped from the soldiers on account of ammunition lost by neglect to the 24th of April, the 16th Light Dragoons to the 21st May, and the 5th line battalion King's German Legion to the 1st of May, may be paid into the hands of the Commissary attached to the brigade in which the regiment is placed.

3. The Commissary will report to the Commissary General when he will have received the money from each regiment.

4. At a General Court Martial, held by virtue of a warrant, and in pursuance of an order from his Excellency Lieutenant General Lord Wellington, K. B. Commander of the Forces, dated Lisbon, 25th April, 1810, of which Major General Leith was President, and Captain Goodman, Deputy Judge Advocate, was arraigned Lieutenant Thomas Crosdale Wilson, of the 9th Light Dragoons, for scandalous, disgraceful, and unmilitary conduct, in forcing a sentry posted on duty whilst in the execution of the particular orders entrusted to him, in the theatre of the Rua des Condes, on or about the evening of the 4th January, 1810.

To which charge the prisoner pleaded not guilty, and the Court proceeded to the examination of witnesses.

OPINION.

The Court having maturely weighed and considered the evidence adduced in support of the prosecution against the prisoner, Lieutenant Thomas Crosdale Wilson, of the 9th Light Dragoons, together with what he has

has offered in his defence, and the evidence thereon, are of opinion, that he is not guilty of the charge preferred against him, and do therefore acquit him of the same. Although from the inconsistency of some parts of the evidence, the Court have not been completely satisfied as to the acts of positive violence having been committed by the Prisoner Lieutenant Wilson, which would have fully established the charge; and as the charge is so worded as to be incapable of subdivision, the course which they have pursued has in their opinion been without any alternative presenting itself, but that of a general acquittal; they cannot however discharge their duty without expressing in the most marked terms their unqualified disapprobation of the conduct of the Prisoner Lieutenant Wilson, which, on the occasion alluded to, appears to have been not only highly disrespectful to the King's service, but subversive of the principles of discipline, by which alone it can be usefully carried on

The Court are therefore of opinion, that if, from the causes before stated, the Prisoner, Lieutenant Wilson, has escaped a sentence of condemnation, he has justly merited that his conduct should be reprobated and censured, the more especially as not only in the occasion alluded to in the charge, but in the loose, indecorous, and generally irrelevant address with which the Prisoner opened his defence, he repays the indulgence of having been permitted to hold at the same time a British and Portuguese commission by denying the authority of his own sovereign to bring him to justice; whilst under an equivocation equally absurd and dangerous, Lieutenant Wilson asserts that as an officer of the Prince Regent, he might with impunity commit every outrage in the midst of the British army employed in the face of an enemy in the field, an assertion so monstrous as to call for the strongest expressions of the disapprobation and censure of the Court, which opinion has been confirmed by his Excellency Lord Viscount Wellington, Commander of the Forces.

5. Lieutenant Wilson is to be released from his arrest, and is to join his regiment.

6. The General Court Martial of which Major General Leith is President is dissolved, and the Members are to return to their duty with their several corps.

7. The Commander of the Forces requests that the order of the 19th May, 1809, may be understood as applying to the horses, &c. brought in by deserters from the enemy; it is desirable and it must be the wish of every officer in the army that these men should have the full benefit which may result from the sales of what they may bring off with them, and therefore their horses, &c. should be allowed to be sold by public auction.

8. Major General Leith is attached to Major General Tilson's brigade in the 2d Division of Infantry; he will take the command of the 2d Division of Infantry under the orders of Lieutenant General Hill.

Adjutant General's Office.

G. O. *Celorico, 22d June,* 1810.

1. At a General Court Martial, assembled by virtue of a warrant and in pursuance of an Order from his Excellency Lord Viscount Wellington, whereof Brigadier General C. Crauford was President, and Captain Conway

 Benning,

Benning, 66th Regiment, Acting Deputy Judge Advocate, held at Portalegre on the 14th June, 1810, was arraigned. Private James Maher, 57th Regiment, on the following charge, viz.

For Desertion from his Regiment at Portalegre, on or about the evening of the 30th May, 1810, with his arms, accoutrements, and necessaries.

OPINION AND SENTENCE.

The Court, having maturely weighed and considered the evidence against the Prisoner James Maher, and what he alleges in his defence, do find him guilty of the crime laid to his charge, being a breach of the Articles of War, and do therefore sentence him, James Maher, Private 1st Bn. 57th Regiment, to be transported for seven years as a felon, and at the expiration of that period to be at the disposal of his Majesty, which sentence has been confirmed by his Excellency the Commander of the Forces.

2. Private James Maher is to be sent to Lisbon in irons by the first opportunity.

ADJUTANT GENERAL'S OFFICE,
Celorico, 22d June, 1810.

G. A. O.

CAPTAIN TUCKER, 29th Regiment, is appointed Commandant of detachments at Belem, and will receive over that charge from Major Lindsay, 39th Regiment.

G. O.

ADJUTANT GENERAL'S OFFICE.

G. O.

Celorico, 23d June, 1810.

Memorandum.—The Paymasters of Regiments in the 3d and Light Divisions of Infantry, and the Hussars, are to send to Almeida to receive the balance due on their estimates to the 24th May, 1810.

The Paymasters of the other Regiments of Cavalry, and of the Regiments in the 1st and 4th Divisions of Infantry, are to send to Celorico for the same purpose.

ADJUTANT GENERAL'S OFFICE.

G. O.

Celorico, 24th June, 1810.

Memorandum.—The Military Departments of Head Quarters will move to Almeida to-morrow.

The Civil Departments are to remain at Celorico.

Memorandum.—Regiments and Corps will make up to the 25th instant, and send to the Adjutant General's Office, as soon after as possible, quarterly Returns of Officers who have been absent without leave for any period during the preceding three months.

Heads of Departments will transmit to the Adjutant General's Office, on or immediately after the 25th instant, a list of Officers at present serving in their respective Departments, and a Memorandum specifying the date of all the appointments and removals that have taken place within the preceding six months.

G. O.

ADJUTANT GENERAL'S OFFICE.

G. O. *Almeida, 29th June, 1810.*

1. HEAD-QUARTERS will move to Alverca to-morrow.

2. The following Generals and Staff Officers have been appointed by his Majesty to serve with the division of the army at present stationed at Cadiz:

	Dates of Appointment.
Lieutenant General Thomas Graham . .	23 Feb. 1810
Captain J. A. Hope, 26th Reg. A. D. C. and Acting Military Secretary	do.
Captain Lord William Russel, 23d L. Dr. A. D. C.	do.
Hon. James Stanhope, 1st Guards, extra do.	24Apr.
Cornet Lord Viscount Ipswich, 7th L. Dr. extra ditto	23Feb.
Lieut. Felix Calvert, 52d Reg. extra ditto	18Apr.
Brigadier General John Sontag	16Mar.
Capt. Edward Fitzgerald, 6th Reg. A. D. C.	do.
—— Charles Tryon, 88th Reg. Brigade Major	2Feb.
Brigadier General D. Hoghton	14Apr.
Captain G. Ramsden, 1st Guards, A. D. C.	1June
—— Neil Douglas, 79th Reg. Brigade Major	26May
Brigadier General W. T. Dilkes . . .	24Feb.
Captain D. Mercer, 3d Guards, A. D. C.	do.

Adjutant

Adjutant General's Department.

Lieut. Col. John Macdonald, Half-pay, 1st Gar. Bat. to be Assistant Adjutant Gen. 24Feb.1810.

Captain Goddard Hare, 23d Reg. Deputy Assistant Adjutant General . . . . . 21do.

Quarter-Master General's Department.

Major Hon. Charles M. Cathcart, Permanent Assistant Quarter-Master General 23do.

Captain John Hamilton, 2d Guards, Deputy Assistant Quarter-Master General . . 2May

Lieut. Isaac Walker, 88th Reg. Acting Deputy Assistant Quarter-Master General 20Mar.

Commissariat Department.

Mathias Delaval O'Meara, Acting Deputy Commissary General 25Dec.1809

William Cumming, Acting Assistant Commissary General 19Mar.1810

James Saumarez Dobree, ditto . . . . 24do.

Edward Robinson, ditto . . . . do.

George Wilgress, ditto . . . . 6do.

Richard Horne, ditto 6May

Thomas Stoneman, ditto . . . . 9do.

Medical Department.

Sir James Fellows, M. D. Director of Hospitals.

Thomas Frederick Nicolay, Acting Deputy Inspector of Hospitals 13Apr.1809

Hugh M'Kay, Staff Surgeon.

John Hume, ditto.

Thomas

Thomas Hume Bowles, Deputy Purveyor to the Forces.

Rev. Mr. Haywood, Chaplain to the Forces.

Captain Daniel Domahoe, 44th Reg. Deputy Judge Advocate 10Apr.1810

Captain Alexander Campbell, 87th Reg. Town Major . . . . 3do.

Captain John Cavendish, Provost Marshal 14do.

Ensign Robert Deane, Assistant ditto . . 21Mar.

Reade, Inspector of Telegraphs.

---

3. Captain Cotton, Deputy Assistant Adjutant General, is attached to the light division of Infantry, vice Captain V. Graham.

4. Captain Radcliffe, of the Royal Dragoons, is appointed to act as Major of Brigade to Major General Slade, till his Majesty's pleasure is known, vice Dance resigned.

Memorandum.—Captain White, 3d Dragoon Guards, will place himself under the orders of Marshal Beresford.

G. O.

ADJUTANT GENERAL'S OFFICE.

G. O. *Alverca, 2d July, 1810.*

1. QUARTER-MASTER-SERJEANT John Stubbs, 2d Battalion 31st Regiment, is appointed an Assistant Provost Marshal to the 2d division of Infantry, *vice* Pass, who resigns.

4. Lieutenant Cheslyn and Lieutenant King, 48th Regiment, will place themselves under the orders of Marshal Beresford.

ADJUTANT GENERAL'S OFFICE.

G. O. *Alverca, 3d July, 1810.*

1. THE General Court Martial, of which Colonel Saunders is President, is adjourned till further orders, and the Members are to return to their duty with their several corps.

Colonel Saunders is to remain at Lisbon for the further orders of the Commander of the Forces.

2. Major the Hon. A. Gordon, 3d Guards, is to resume his situation as Extra Aide-de-Camp to his Excellency the Commander of the Forces.

3. Mr. Assistant Commissary-General Ruth is attached to the Cavalry as senior Commissariat officer of that division. The following persons late Store-keepers in the Commissariat are discharged from that department.

Messrs. Gibbons
Collins
Cooper, Sen.
Rees
Callow

ADJUTANT GENERAL'S OFFICE.

G. A. O. *Alverca, 3d July,* 1810.

THE Pay Masters of regiments are as soon as possible to attend at Celerico, to receive the balances of their estimates to the 24th June.

Memorandum.—Lieutenant Managan of the Buffs has permission to serve with the Portuguese army, and will report himself forthwith to Marshal Beresford.

ADJUTANT GENERAL'S OFFICE.

G. O. *Alverca, 4th July,* 1810.

Memorandum.—CAPTAIN Dance, 23d Lt. Dragoons, will place himself under the orders of Marshal Beresford.

ADJUTANT GENERAL'S OFFICE.

G. O. *Alverca, 5th July,* 1810.

Memorandum.—CAPT. Dawkins, Coldstream Guards, is appointed Brigade Major to the Brigade of Guards from the 23d April, 1810.

ADJUTANT GENERAL'S OFFICE.

G. O. *Alverca, 6th July,* 1810.

1. THE Commander of the Forces is concerned to notice the frequent omissions of the regiments to send proper returns of the Necessaries, &c. of the soldiers to the General

ral Hospital along with them, the consequence of which is, that the Purveyors of the Hospital cannot be responsible for the Necessaries of the men.

They are referred to the General Orders, 17th December, 1809, in which it will be observed, that a Report is required to be made to the General Officer commanding the Brigade that it has been obeyed.

2. As it appears that the Necessaries of several men, particularly 1st Battalion 11th Regiment, were found deficient, in addition to the men who were sent in without proper returns, an Officer of the 11th is to proceed to Coimbra forthwith to inquire into the circumstances which occasioned the deficiences.

3. The Adjutant General will send to the Commanding Officers the List of the names of the men, and the deficiences of each.

4. As it appears from comparing at the Adjutant General's Office the division orderly books with the general orderly book of the army, that various omissions and mistakes have arisen, it becomes necessary to call the attention of the Officers of the Department very particularly to the future regularity of the General Orders issued by them to the different divisions.

5. It has been conceived by some gentlemen that the orderly books were their own property, and on the removal of an officer of the Department from one division to another, they have thought themselves entitled to the orderly book of the division they served in.

6. It is the Commander of the Forces' positive directions, that the orderly books now belonging to each division are never to be carried away, or exchanged, but to be considered as wholly appertaining to the division; and if it

 should

should be broken up or divided, the Officer of the Department in charge of the orderly books will apply to the Adjutant General's Office for instructions concerning them.

7. The Officers of the Department must enter the General Orders into the orderly book themselves and not entrust them to a clerk. They must sign their names at the bottom of each day's orders, as being responsible for the entry.

8. The General Orders are to be kept at one end of the book and the Division Orders at the other, when they meet, a new book is to be procured, which is charged in the contingent account. This will facilitate the comparing the General Orders.

9. Division orderly books will be called for every two months to be compared, and returned with the Adjutant General's signature as being correct: any errors the Officers of the Department will have to repair to Head Quarters to correct.

10. Division Officers of the Department will call for in the same manner the Brigade Major's orderly books, and compare them with their's.

11. Officers of the Department are not only to acknowledge the receipt of General Orders, but they are to make a particular report, on the 1st and 14th of every Month, of the days upon which no General Orders have been received, addressed to the Adjutant General.

12. General Officers commanding divisions will please to see these orders strictly complied with.

ADJUTANT GENERAL'S OFFICE.

G. O. *Alverca, 9th July,* 1810.

1. Pay Masters of regiments and other Officers, who have

have money to pay to the Commissary General on account either of necessaries furnished to the Regiments, or any other account, are to pay it, on account of the Commissary General, into the hands of the Deputy Paymaster General, and take his receipt for the same.

2. The receipt of the Deputy Paymaster General is then to be taken to the Office of the Commissary General at Head-Quarters, and exchanged for the receipt of the Commissary General, which can alone be the discharge for the sum due.

3. Serjeant Crain, 74th Regiment, is appointed an Assistant Provost, and will repair to Head-Quarters immediately for instructions.

ADJUTANT GENERAL'S OFFICE.

G. O. *11th July*, 1810.

1. THE Commander of the Forces requests that the General Officers commanding divisions will direct that those soldiers, who may be inclined to reap the harvest may have leave of absence for that purpose.

ADJUTANT GENERAL'S OFFICE.

G. O. *Alverca, 12th July*, 1810.

1. CAPTAIN Brownrig, 52d Regiment, is appointed an extra Aide-de-Camp to Lieutenant General Sir Brent Spencer, K. B.

2. The Commanding Officer of the 11th Regiment will report the reason for which Joseph Thatcher of that Regiment was sent to the Hospital at Coimbra without a

list of necessaries, and Brigadier General Campbell is requested to state whether any report was made to him respecting this man under the orders of 17th December, 1809, No. 5.

ADJUTANT GENERAL'S OFFICE.

G. O. *Alverca*, 13*th July*, 1810.

1. THE men, according to the return underneath, were deficient in necessaries when sent to the General Hospital on the 6th instant.

These men have declared, what the Commander of the Forces is disinclined to believe, that the returns of their necessaries were made without a previous inspection by the officers of the companies to which they belong.

The General Officers commanding brigades are requested to inquire into this circumstance.

FOURTH DIVISION, INFANTRY.

List of Soldiers who entered the General Hospital on 6th July, 1810.

7th Regiment, John Evans
——————— John Duffy
97th Regiment, Patrick Casey
——————— John Bryerly
——————— Joseph Gratzo
——————— Andrew Hanaly
40th Regiment, William Warren
——————— John Pratt
——————— David Williams

11th

11th Regiment, Henry Pearse
———— Patrick Farrell
———— John Dougherty
———— Michael Singleton
———— William Watts
———— Samuel Holloway
———— John Robinson
———— Richard Huckstable

The further particulars of the return are sent to the regiments concerned.

2. Acting Assistant Commissary General Hodges is attached to the brigade commanded by Major General Leith.

ADJUTANT GENERAL'S OFFICE.

G. O. *Alverca, 14th July*, 1810.

1. PAYMASTERS of Regiments are to send to Celorico to-morrow, to receive a part of the balance on their estimates to the 24th July, and the contingencies to the 24th June.

ADJUTANT GENERAL'S OFFICE.

G. O. *Alverca, 17th July*, 1810.

1. CAPTAIN Selby Smith of the Royals is appointed to act as Major of Brigade to the brigade of infantry consisting of the

3d Battalion, Royals.
1st Ditto 9th Regiment.
2d Ditto 38th Regiment.

 2. Serjeant

2. Serjeant Richard Newman of the Royals is appointed an Assistant Provost Marshal to the division commanded by Major General Leith.

ADJUTANT GENERAL'S OFFICE,
G. O. *Alverca, 18th July*, 1810.

1. CAPTAIN Robert Brownrig, 52d Regiment, is to act as a Deputy Assistant Quarter Master General until His Majesty's pleasure is known.

ADJUTANT GENERAL'S OFFICE.
G. O. *Alverca, 20th July*, 1810.

1. THE Commander of the Forces requests that when commanding officers of regiments, brigades, or divisions, think it proper to order that any of the troops should fire by way of practice, they will give notice of their intention to fire to the detachments of troops which may be cantoned in their neighbourhood.

ADJUTANT GENERAL'S OFFICE.
G. O. *Alverca, 21st July*, 1810.

1. THE officer commanding 1st Battalion, 3d Regiment, will report the manner in which four men of that regiment came to be returned missing from that battalion in the Weekly State of the 15th July, beyond the number of missing returned in the former states.

2. The

2. The Commander of the Forces requests that the officer commanding the brigade in which the 1st Battalion, Buffs, is placed, will report whether the officer commanding that regiment obeyed the order of the 29th May, 1809, regarding those men.

3. The officers of the corps of the Royal Engineers are posted to the divisions of the army as follows;

Lieutenant General Sir Brent Spencer's Division—
Captain Goldfinch.
Lieutenant Thompson.

Lieutenant General Hill's Divisiou—
Captain Squire.

Major General Picton's Division—
Captain Burgoyne.

Major General the Hon. Lowrey Cole's Division—
Captain Mulcaster.

Major General Leith's Corps—
Captain Ross.

Light Division—
Captain Williams.

ADJUTANT GENERAL'S OFFICE.

G. O. *Alverca, 23d July,* 1810.

A BOARD, consisting of one Field Officer and two Captains, from the Brigade of Guards, will assemble at Celorico to examine and report upon the state of a considerable quantity of damaged flour and biscuit.

G. O.

ADJUTANT GENERAL'S OFFICE.

G.O. *Alverca, 24th July, 1810.*

1. THE officers commanding detachments proceeding to the army must conform to all the regulations in respect to sending men into General Hospital, which are laid down for the conduct of the regiments by the different General Orders.

2. The following men belonging to detachments were sent into the Hospital at Coimbra without a list of necessaries:

Robert Atkinson, 7th Regiment.

John Hayles, 1st Bn. 45th Regiment.

3. The man undermentioned was admitted on the 14th into the Hospital at Coimbra, from a detachment coming from Figuera, without a List of Necessaries :

John O'Brian, 2d Bn. 5th Regiment.

4. The Commander of the Forces repeats that he considers the Assistant Adjutant General at Lisbon, and the Commanding Officer of the detachments at Belem, to be responsible that the officers proceeding in command of detachments from Lisbon are made acquainted with the General Orders which have been given out at different times for their guidance.

5. The Commander of the Forces is concerned to publish the following details of a murder committed by the troops near Guarda.

6. In the night between the 10th and 11th of July, a single farm-house within two miles of Guarda was broken open by soldiers, who murdered the man of the house and a girl of about 8 years of age, and wounded the mother dangerously in the head.

This

This horrid act appears to have been committed with an axe, which belonged to the house, and was by the murderers left in it. The woman survived, and states that the soldiers, who entered the house by breaking open a window, were six or seven in number, and that they were dressed in white trowsers, red coats, and buff or yellow facings; after committing the murder, the soldiers robbed the house of about twelve dollars, some gold bead necklaces and ear-rings.

7. The Commander of the Forces has no doubt that the measures he has adopted will soon discover to him who committed this horrid murder; but that the murderers may not any longer enjoy the fruits of their crime unpunished, he hereby offers a reward of 50 dollars and a pardon to any person who will give information to produce the conviction of the murderers.

8. The Commander of the Forces repeats that he is convinced, if the non-commissioned officers did their duty, these crimes could not be committed by the soldiers without their knowledge. It is incumbent upon those belonging to the regiments stationed at Guarda whose uniforms have been described, to exert themselves to discover who committed this shocking murder.

ADJUTANT GENERAL'S OFFICE.

G. O. *Alverca, 26th July,* 1810.

Extract of a Letter from the Earl of Liverpool to Lord Viscount Wellington, dated Downing Street, 26th June, 1810.

I TAKE this opportunity of answering the query contained in your Lordship's letter of 6th April, relative

relative to the amount of Stoppage (if any, "that is to be made from the pay of the non-commissioned officers and privates who might regain their liberty in Spain") during the time that they remained prisoners in the enemy's hands. The subject having been referred to the Secretary at War, it has been determined that 6d. a day should be stopped from the full pay of each man from the day of his being taken up to that on which he should actually rejoin a British corps.

ADJUTANT GENERAL'S OFFICE.

G. O. *Alverca, 27th July,* 1810.

1. THE Commander of the Forces requests that the General Officers commanding divisions and brigades, and the Officers commanding regiments, will invariably adopt effectual measures to prevent the streets of the towns in which they may be cantoned, or the roads in the neighbourhood of their cantonments, from being choked up with baggage, with carriages, or otherwise.

2. All carriages and loaded animals on their march must, when halted, if only for a short period, be packed in a field in the neighbourhood of the high road, or housed, but must not on any account be left in the streets of any village, or on the road.

3. When a regiment on its march is halted for any length of time, or when halted is bivouaced, the soldiers must not be permitted to sit or lie down upon the road, but must be placed on one side of it.

4. The officers commanding detachments with baggage, or carriages of any description, the conductors of ordnance or

or commissariat stores, and the officers commanding regiments, are responsible for a strict obedience to this order.

5. The general and other officers of the army will see the necessity of an early and strict obedience to the orders of the army, respecting the marching, cantoning, and provisioning of the troops, and to the preservation of order and discipline, as well as those which may be issued for the operations of the troops.

6. Major General the Honourable William Stewart is appointed to command the brigade heretofore under the orders of Major General Tilson.

ADJUTANT GENERAL'S OFFICE.
A. G. O. *Alverca, 27th July,* 1810.

CORNET the Earl of March, 13th Light Dragoons, is appointed an extra Aide-de-Camp to the Commander of the Forces.

ADJUTANT GENERAL'S OFFICE.
G. O. *Celorico, 29th July,* 1810.

HORSE GUARDS.
6th July, 1810.

MY LORD,

1. HAVING had the honour to lay before the King the proceedings of a General Court Martial held at Lisbon on the 21st and 22d of May, 1810, for the trial of Hospital Mate Daniel Maginn, who was arraigned upon the under-mentioned charges, namely:

For

For highly mutinous, scandalous, and infamous conduct, such as unbecoming the character of an officer and a gentleman, in grossly insulting and striking Lieutenant Dunkin of the 4th Dragoons, his superior officer, while in command on board the Anacreon Transport, when on the passage from England to Portugal, on or about the month of February or March, 1810; on which charges the Court came to the following decision:

The Court having maturely weighed and considered the evidence adduced in support of the prosecution against the prisoner, Hospital Mate Daniel Maginn, together with what he has urged in his defence, and the evidence thereon, are of opinion that he is guilty of the charge preferred against him, (being in breach of the Articles of War,) and do by virtue thereof sentence him the prisoner, Hospital Mate Daniel Maginn, to be cashiered. The Court cannot close its proceedings without noticing the extremely reprehensible conduct of Lieutenant Dunkin during his command on board the Anacreon Transport, and which appears to them, in a great measure, to have given rise to the unjustifiable occurrence which took place on the passage to this country.

I am to acquaint your Lordship that His Majesty was pleased to approve and confirm the finding and sentence of the Court; your Lordship will therefore acquaint me with the day on which the sentence is made known to the prisoner, Hospital Mate Daniel Maginn, as from that day he will cease to receive pay in His Majesty's service.

(Signed) DAVID DUNDAS,
Commander in Chief.

Lieutenant General
Lord Viscount Wellington, K. B.
&c. &c. &c.

HORSE GUARDS,
6th July, 1810.

MY LORD,

2. HAVING had the honour to lay before the King the Proceedings of a General Court Martial held at Lisbon on the 14th of May, 1810, and continued by adjournment to the 19th of the same month, for the trial of Hospital Mate James Malony, who was arraigned on the undermentioned Charges, viz.

1st, For highly mutinous, scandalous, and infamous conduct, such as unbecoming the character of an officer and a gentleman, in grossly insulting and striking Lieutenant Dunkin of the 4th Dragoons, his superior officer, while in command on board the Anacreon Transport, when on the passage from England to Portugal, on or about the month of February or March, 1810.

2d, For most scandalous, infamous, and disgraceful conduct, such as unbecoming the character of an officer and a gentleman, in grossly insulting and striking Ensign M'Lean of the 5th Foot, his superior officer, when on board the said Anacreon Transport, on or about the month of February or March, 1810.

Upon which Charges the Court came to the following decision:

The Court having maturely and deliberately weighed and considered the evidence adduced in support of the prosecution against the prisoner, Hospital Mate James Malony, together with what he brought forward in his defence, and the evidence thereon, are of opinion, he is guilty of the charges preferred against him, (being in breach of the Articles of War,) and do by virtue thereof sentence him, the prisoner, Hospital Mate James Malo-

ny,

ny, to be cashiered. The Court are induced to pass this lenient sentence in consideration of the inexperience of the Prisoner in the very short period of his service.

I am to acquaint your Lordship that His Majesty was pleased to approve and confirm the finding and sentence of the Court. Your Lordship will therefore acquaint me with the day upon which the Sentence is made known to the prisoner, Hospital Mate James Malony, as from that day he will cease to receive pay in His Majesty's service.

(Signed) DAVID DUNDAS,
Commander in Chief.

Lieutenant General
Lord Viscount Wellington, K. B.
&c. &c. &c.

3. Captain Alexander M'Dougall, of the 5th Regiment, is appointed to act as supernumerary Aide-de-Camp to Brigadier General A. Campbell.

4. The Commander of the Forces observes that notwithstanding repeated orders upon the subject, nearly all the regiments of the army have cars in their possession carrying baggage and attended by soldiers. He refrains upon this occasion from taking any further notice of this irregularity, but if he should see hereafter a cart drawn by bullocks in any part of the line of march of the troops, orders will be given that the baggage shall be destroyed, and the officer to whom it belongs will be brought before a General Court Martial.

5. The Commander of the Forces observed yesterday that several men of the Hanoverian Legion were straggling from their corps, he requests that Brigadier General Low will report what number of men were reported ab-

sent

sent from each regiment after the march of yesterday, and the cause of their absence.

6. The Paymasters of Regiments will proceed to the neighbourhood of Penhancos to receive the amount of their Estimates up to the 24th of July, 1810.

ADJUTANT GENERAL'S OFFICE.

A. G. O. *Celorico, 29th July,* 1810.

THE sick of the different divisions and brigades of the army will, until further orders, be sent by Villa Cortes, Penhancos, Chamusca, and Venda de Valle, to Farinha de Porre, where the General Hospital will be established.

ADJUTANT GENERAL'S OFFICE.

G. O. *Celorico, 30th July,* 1810.

Memorandum.—Lieutenant Armstrong, 11th Foot, will place himself under the orders of Marshal Beresford.

The General Order of the 16th November, 1809, directing Ensign Power, 97th Regiment, to place himself under the orders of Marshal Beresford, is cancelled.

ADJUTANT GENERAL'S OFFICE.

G. O. *Celorico, 31st July,* 1810.

1. Mr. Daniel Ibbetson,
Mr. James Laidley,
Mr. John Peter Housten,

 are

are appointed to act as Deputy Assistant Commissaries till His Majesty's pleasure is known.

2. The Deputy Judge Advocate is appointed to act as a Deputy Assistant in the Adjutant General's Department, but without pay or emolument.

ADJUTANT GENERAL'S OFFICE.

G. O. *Celorico, 1st August*, 1810.

1. THE following Orders and Rules are to be observed respecting communications with the enemy's out-posts.

2. No flag of truce must be sent to the Enemy without orders from the Commander of the Forces.

3. No letter, or other communication, must be sent by a flag of truce which has been ordered by the Commander of the Forces, unless such letter has first been transmitted to Head Quarters, and it must be open.

4. Flags of truce from the enemy must be received by the Officer commanding the first post at which they will arrive. The Officer commanding the post is to receive the flag of truce, or Officer coming with it, to take from him the letter or communication with which he will be charged, and to give him a receipt for it, and he is then to send him back again to his own lines.

5. The simplicity and indiscretion with which communications have been made to the enemy respecting the positions, &c. of this army and other circumstances, render these orders absolutely necessary, and the Commander of the Forces trusts that the Officers commanding at the outpicquets, who may have to receive the enemy's flags, will confine their conversation entirely to the subject on which they

they are to communicate, viz. the receipt of the letter or message from the enemy, and the immediate departure of the officer delivering it.

6. Lieutenant Colonel Elly, Assistant Adjutant General, having returned from leave of absence, will resume his situation with the cavalry division.

ADJUTANT GENERAL'S OFFICE.

G. O. *Celorico, 2d August,* 1810.

1. THE Commander of the Forces requests that the Officers of the Staff, and the Infantry of the Army will not employ the farriers of the Cavalry to shoe their horses.

2. The farriers of the Cavalry must be employed solely in making shoes and shoeing the horses belonging to the Cavalry.

ADJUTANT GENERAL'S OFFICE,

G. O. *Celorico, 3d August,* 1810.

1. IN case the General Officers commanding Divisions should find it necessary to make any alteration in the distribution of the Portuguese Troops in their Division, they are requested to apprize Colonel D'Urban, Quarter Master General of the Portuguese Army, thereof, as well as the Quarter Master General of the British Army, in order that the Portuguese Commissariat may be able to take measures to supply the Troops.

2. A Court of Enquiry will assemble this day at two o'clock, consisting of Lieutenant Colonel Beckwith,

President,

President, and two Captains of the Light Division, to investigate the circumstances of several articles of church plate having been found in the baggage of a Storekeeper (of the name of Haydon) attached to the Light Division.

ADJUTANT GENERAL'S OFFICE,
G. O. *Celorico, 4th August,* 1810.

1. A GENERAL Court Martial will immediately assemble at Guarda for the trial of such Prisoners as may be brought before it.

Colonel Kemmis, President.

The Members to be furnished by the 40th, 27th, and 97th Regiments.

2. The Light Division is to be divided into two Brigades, viz. the 43d Regiment, 3d Caçadores, and four Companies 95th Regiment, in one Brigade.

The 52d Regiment, 1st Caçadores, and four Companies 95th Regiment, in the other Brigade.

Lieutenant Colonel Beckwith, of the 95th, is to command the Brigade consisting of the

43d Regiment,
3d Caçadores,
4 Companies, 95th Regiment.

Lieutenant Colonel Barclay, of the 52d, is to command the Brigade consisting of the

52d Regiment,
1st Caçadores,
4 Companies 95th Regiment.

---

4. When

4. When a Lieutenant Colonel of a Regiment is announced in General Orders to command a Brigade of which the Regiment under his command forms part, he is to receive a staff allowance of Lieutenant Colonel on the Staff equal to the subsistence of his rank.

5. Lieutenant Colonel Barnes, of the Royals, is to command the Brigade of British Infantry consisting of the

3d Battalion, Royals,
1st do. . . . 9th Regiment,
2d do. . . . 38th Regiment.

---

6. Lieutenant Colonel Lord Blantyre is to command the Brigade of Infantry consisting of the

2d Battalion, 24th Regiment,
2d do. . . . 42d Regiment,
1st do. . . . 61st Regiment,

during the absence of Brigadier General Cameron.

---

7. The Commander of the Forces has frequently had occasion to complain of the inconvenience which resulted to the public service from the practice which prevails of Officers and Soldiers pressing carriages of the country by their own authority, and this inconvenience has been again felt in an aggravated degree in consequence of the pressing of carriages, in a recent instance, by a conductor of stores, Peter Conroy; he requests the Commanding Officer of Artillery will report what occasion this conductor had for carriages, and will cause strict inquiry to be made, whether, before he pressed these carriages, he made application for them to any British Commissary or Magistrate of the country, and will report whether Conductor Conroy had made any report of his having pressed these carriages.

8. It is impossible to carry on the service if these irregularities are persevered in, and the Commander of the Forces is determined to punish, in this, and in every other instance, any disobedience of his repeated orders upon this subject.

ADJUTANT GENERAL'S OFFICE.

G. O. *Celorico, 5th August,* 1810.

1. THOSE Officers and Regiments which have not received their bât and forage are to apply to the Commissary General for it, who will give them orders upon the Paymaster General for the amount, which orders they are to present for payment near Penhancos without loss of time.

ADJUTANT GENERAL'S OFFICE.

A. G. O. *Celorico, 5th August,* 1810.

AT a General Court Martial held at Guarda by virtue of a warrant and in pursuance of an order from his Excellency Lieutenant General Lord Viscount Wellington, K. B. on the 4th of August, 1810, of which Colonel Kemmis, of the 40th Regiment, was President, and Captain Goodman, 48th Regiment, Deputy Judge Advocate, Privates John Linahan and Albert Mackovitz, of the 97th Regiment, were arraigned—

For deserting from their Regiment towards the enemy on or about the 31st July and the morning of the 1st August, 1810.

The

The Prisoners pleaded not guilty, and the Court proceeded to the examination of witnesses; and having maturely considered the evidence and what the Prisoners offered in their defence, were of opinion that they are both Guilty of the charge preferred against them, and do sentence them the Prisoners, Privates John Linahan and Albert Mackovitz, of the 97th Regiment, to be shot to death, at such time and place as his Excellency the Commander of the Forces may think fit.

Which Sentence has been confirmed by his Excellency the Commander of the Forces.

The Sentence of the General Court Martial on the trial of John Linahan and Albert Mackovitz, of the 97th Regiment, is to be carried into execution on Monday morning the 6th instant, in presence of the troops stationed at Guarda, to be paraded for that purpose, by a detachment of the 97th Regiment, under the direction of the Assistant Provost of the 4th Division.

The General Court Martial, of which Colonel Kemmis is President, is dissolved, and the Members are to return to their duty.

ADJUTANT GENERAL'S OFFICE,

G. O. *Celorico, 6th August,* 1810.

1. BRIGADE Major Rowan is attached to the Light Brigade under the command of Lieutenant Colonel Barclay.

Lieutenant Stewart, 95th Regiment, is appointed to act as Brigade Major till his Majesty's pleasure is known, and is attached to the Light Brigade under the command of Lieutenant Colonel Beckwith.

 3. Lieutenant

3. Lieutenant Bell, 52d Regiment, is attached as a Deputy Assistant to the Department of the Quarter Master General till his Majesty's pleasure is known.

ADJUTANT GENERAL'S OFFICE,

G. O. *Celorico, 7th August,* 1810.

1. PAYMASTERS of Regiments are to go to the Paymaster General near Penhancos to receive one half of the subsistence due on their estimates to the 24th instant.

ADJUTANT GENERAL'S OFFICE.

G. O. *Celorico, 8th August,* 1810.

1. THE order No. 6. of the 27th July, ought to be as follows:

Major General the Honorable William Stewart is attached to Major General Tilson's Brigade in the 2d division of Infantry. He will take the Command of the 2d division of Infantry, under the orders of Lieutenant General Hill.

Memorandum.—The following Officers of the 2d battalion Royal Fusileers will join forthwith the 1st battalion of that Regiment.

Captain Crowder,
Lieutenant Hammerton,
——— Davy,
——— Anderson,
——— Ormsby,
——— Morgan.

G. O.

ADJUTANT GENERAL'S OFFICE.

G. O. *Celorico, 10th August*, 1810.

1. EXTRACT of a letter from Vice Admiral Berkeley, dated Lisbon, 6th August, 1810.

2. The Commander of the forces publishes to the army, the extract of a letter from Admiral Berkeley, and its enclosures.

3. I cannot but think it my duty to transmit the copy of a letter from the Vice Consul at Oporto, to the Commander of His Majesty's cutter the Dart, enclosing extracts of two letters; the contents of which I shall not venture to comment upon, except that it has thrown that place into such dismay, and consternation, that I have had official application for Ships of war, &c. to take off the inhabitants. Colonel Trant may possibly gain some clue to the writer, by referring to the Merchant mentioned in the Consul's letter.

4. Copy of a letter from John Alvay, Esq. His Britannic Majesty's Consul at Oporto to Lieutenant Cross, Commanding His Majesty's cutter Dart.

Oporto, 1st August, 1810.

SIR,

SINCE my respects to you this morning, I beg leave to enclose an abstract of a letter from a British Officer of rank to Mr. John Tindall, a respectable British Merchant here, by which you will see the critical situation we are at present placed in. I therefore request in my name, as well as that of the British Merchants here, that you will take into consideration the necessity of your remaining off this Bar, (being compatible with the orders you have received) to afford protection to such British vessels

vessels as may be ready to sail, as well as to any British subjects, who may from more imminent danger, be under the necessity of suddenly embarking.

I yesterday received a letter from the Commissary General at Lisbon dated the 28th, who mentioned the Growler gun brig had sailed from thence for this place, but as yet has not appeared. We are in great consternation, and unanimously request your compliance.

I am, Sir,

Your most obedient,

(Signed) JOHN ALVAY, Consul.

To Lieutenant Cross,

Commanding His Majesty's cutter Dart.

5. Abstract alluded to in the foregoing letter, dated Penhancos, 28th July, 1810.—We are just arrived here—The guards, and General Cameron's division that was, 42d, 24th, and 61st, are arrived at St. Payo, and Gouvea; Lord Wellington's Head-Quarters are to be at Celorico this evening; but it is said that General Cole still remains at Guarda. I have seen some of the Staff, who tell me that the whole force under Massena, Regnier's included, amounts to 105,000 men, 40 Regiments of which are Cavalry; 86,000 are marching on our rear; you will hardly suppose that Lord Wellington will make a stand against such a force, and we must retreat, and eventually leave the country.

Torsillo, 28 Leagues from Oporto.

6. It is now said that we shall retreat until we come to the bridge of Murcella, 4 leagues from Coimbra, where it is thought we shall make our first stand; Engineers, I know, are gone down to mine the bridge for explosion; 24,000 rations of biscuit are to arrive there this evening; various

various are the conjectures; but all agree in supposing it would be madness to think of contending unsuccessfully with Massena's army, and really, until we form a junction of our whole force, I think we shall not make a stand. Thomar and Villa Franca is the most likely—partial skirmishes we expect daily. The flying artillery and heavy dragoons have moved up to Celorico to protect the retreat of the rear.

7. The Commander of the forces will not make any enquiry to discover the writer of the letters which have occasioned this unnecessary alarm in a quarter in which it was most desirable it should not be created. He has frequently lamented the ignorance which has appeared in the opinions communicated in letters written from the army, and the indiscretion with which those letters are published.

It is impossible that many officers of the army can have a knowledge of facts to enable them to form opinions of the probable events of the campaign; but their opinions, however erroneous, must, when published, have mischievous effects.

8. The communication of that, of which all officers have a knowledge, viz. the numbers and disposition of the different divisions of the army, and of its magazines, is still more mischievous than the communication of opinions, as must be obvious to those who reflect that the army has been for months in the same position; and it is a fact come to the knowledge of the Commander of the Forces, that the plans of the enemy have been founded on information of this description extracted from the English newspapers, which information must have been obtained through private letters from officers of the army.

9. Although

9. Although the difficulties inseparable from the situation of every army engaged in operations in the field, particularly in those of a defensive nature, are much aggravated by communications of this description, the Commander of the Forces only requests that the officers will for the sake of their own reputations, avoid to give opinions upon which they cannot have a knowledge to enable them to form any, and that if they choose to communicate facts to their correspondents, regarding the positions of the army, its numbers, formation of its magazines, preparations for breaking bridges, &c. they will urge their correspondents not to publish their letters in the newspapers until it shall be certain that the publication of the intelligence will not be injurious to the army, or to the public service.

Adjutant General's Office.

G. O. *Celorico, 11th August,* 1810.

1. The Commander of the Forces wishes that the General Orders of the 17th June, 1809, regarding the mode of cutting and procuring green forage, may be considered applicable to the unthrashed corn required for the use of the horses of the army.

2. In cases, in which the owner of the unthrashed corn, or the magistrate of the village, is not on the spot to take the receipt or payment of what is required, a Commissary, or Quarter Master, is to keep a note of the quantity taken from the neighbourhood of each village on each day.

3. It is to be understood that when ripe unthrashed corn of any description is issued to the horses of the army, it is in lieu of an equal weight of straw and corn, and 24 pounds

pounds are to be considered the full ration of unthrashed corn of any description.

4. Captain Egerton of the 34th Regiment is to act as a Deputy Assistant in the Department of the Adjutant General, till His Majesty's pleasure is known, and is attached to the corps of troops under the command of Lieutenant General Hill.

5. A General Court Martial will assemble on Tuesday, the 14th instant, at Mello, to try such prisoners as shall be brought before it.

Major General Lightburne, President.

The Members to be furnished equally by the 1st and 3d Divisions.

ADJUTANT GENERAL'S OFFICE.

G. O. *Celorico, 12th August,* 1810.

1. LIEUTENANT Colonel Spry of the 77th Regiment, being arrived in Portugal, will place himself under the orders of Marshal Beresford.

2. Lieutenant Heathcote of the Royal Dragoons is attached as a Deputy Assistant to the Department of the Quarter Master General till His Majesty's pleasure is known.

ADJUTANT GENERAL'S OFFICE.

G. O. *Celorico, 14th August,* 1810.

2. THE undermentioned Officers of the Commissariat Department have joined the army.

Deputy Commissary General John Thompson,
Ditto. Ditto. James Pipon,
Ditto. Ditto. James Ramsey Cooper.

3. Serjeant

3. Serjeant Simms of the Royal Dragoons is appointed an Assistant Provost Marshal to the army, and is attached to the cavalry division.

ADJUTANT GENERAL'S OFFICE.

G. O. *Celorico, 15th August,* 1810.

1. COLONEL Saunders of the 61st Regiment is appointed a Colonel on the Staff till His Majesty's pleasure is known.

ADJUTANT GENERAL'S OFFICE.

G. O. *Alverca, 17th August,* 1810.

1. AT a General Court Martial, held by virtue of a Warrant, and in pursuance of an order from His Excellency Lieutenant General Lord Viscount Wellington, K. B. Commander of the Forces, of which Major General Lightburne was President, and Captain Goodman, 48th Regiment, Deputy Judge Advocate, which was held at Mello, 14th August, 1810, Lieutenant Francis Guilhermy was arraigned for scandalous and infamous conduct, unbecoming the character of an officer and a gentleman, in grossly insulting and ill-treating Lieutenant Briscoe of the 97th Regiment, on or about the 2d and 3d days of July, 1810.

The Court having maturely considered the evidence in support of the prosecution, and what was brought forward by the Prisoner in his defence, was of opinion he is guilty of part of the charge preferred against him, viz.

Ill-treating Lieutenant Briscoe of the 97th Regiment, on or about the 3d day of July, 1810, being in breach of the Articles of War, and do therefore sentence him to be suspended from rank and pay for the space of six calendar months.

The

The Court is further of opinion that the Prisoner, Lieutenant Francis Guilhermy, 97th Regiment, is not guilty of scandalous and infamous conduct, unbecoming the character of an officer and a gentleman, in grossly insulting Lieutenant Briscoe, on or about the 2d and 3d days of July, 1810, and do acquit him of the same.

The Court are induced to pass this lenient sentence in consequence of the provocation the Prisoner received from Lieutenant Briscoe, which sentence has been confirmed by His Excellency the Commander of the Forces.

2. At the same General Court Martial, and on the 14th day of August, Private Alexander Cameron, 2d Battalion, 42d Regiment, was arraigned for repeated desertions, particularly on or about the 2d February, 1810.

The Court having maturely considered the evidence in support of the prosecution, and what the Prisoner offered in his defence, are of opinion that he is guilty of the charge preferred against him, being in breach of the Articles of War, and do therefore sentence him to be transported as a felon for the space of seven years, and at the expiration of such term of years to be at the disposal of His Majesty to serve as a soldier in any of His Majesty's forces, at home or abroad, for life, or otherwise, as His Majesty shall think fit.

Which sentence has been confirmed by His Excellency the Commander of the Forces.

3. At the same General Court Martial, and on the 15th day of August, 1810, Thomas Smyth, Private, servant to Assistant Commissary Sawyer, and a follower of the army, was arraigned for robbing his master of a sum of £106 sterling or thereabouts, at or near Formosa de Salvador, on or about the 19th July, 1810.

The

The Court having maturely considered the evidence, and what the Prisoner offered in his defence, were of opinion, he is guilty of the charge exhibited against him, being in breach of the Articles of War, and do by virtue thereof sentence him, the Prisoner, Thomas Smyth, follower of the army, to be hanged by the neck till dead, at such time and place as His Excellency the Commander of the Forces may think fit.

Which sentence has been confirmed by His Excellency the Commander of the Forces.

4. At the same General Court Martial, and on the 17th day of August, 1810, Private John Hands of the 43d Regiment, was arraigned, for attempting to desert towards the enemy, at or near Moline das Flores, on or about the 19th June, 1810.

The Court having considered the evidence against the Prisoner, together with what he offered in his defence, were of opinion, he was guilty of the charge exhibited against him, being in breach of the Articles of War, and do by virtue thereof sentence him, the Prisoner, Private John Hands, 43d Regiment, to be shot to death, at such time and place as His Excellency the Commander of the Forces shall think fit.

Which sentence has been confirmed by His Excellency the Commander of the Forces.

5. The sentence of the General Court Martial on Lieutenant Guilhermy, 97th Regiment, is to take effect from this day.

6. Private Alexander Cameron of the 2d Battalion, 42d Regiment, is to be sent to Lisbon in irons by the first opportunity.

7. The sentence of the General Court Martial on Thomas

mas Smyth, follower of the army, is to be carried into execution, at Celorico, by the Assistant Provost at that station, on Monday, the 20th August.

8. The sentence of the General Court Martial on the prisoner, John Hands, 43d Regiment, is to be carried into execution in the presence of the 43d Regiment and the other Troops of the Light Divisoin at the same station, to be paraded for that purpose, on to-morrow evening, by a party of the 43d Regiment, under the direction of the Assistant Provost attached to the Light Division.

9. Proceedings of a Medical Board held by order of Abraham Bolton, Deputy Inspector of Hospitals, at Lisbon, 14th August, 1810, to report upon the state of health of Lieutenant Burke, 97th Regiment, and upon his capability of his immediately joining his regiment.

Doctor Summers, M. D. President.

Members.

Louis Krazeitsen } Staff Surgeons.
Charles Maypother }

The Board having met and minutely examined into the state of health of Lieutenant Burke, find, that he labours under an inveterate swelling of his left testicle, which has now become schirrous, accompanied by a virulent eruption upon his thighs and legs.

He is at present certainly not fit to join his regiment, nor is it possible for the Board to determine, when he may be equal to regimental duty; but the Board take leave to observe, that Lieutenant Burke appears to have neglected the means of re-establishing his health.

10. The Commander of the Forces is astonished, that any Officer should neglect the means of re-establishing his

 health

health at the present moment, in the circumstances in which the army is placed.

Lieutenant Burke, of the 97th Regiment, is to remain in his quarters, and the medical Officer who attends him is to report on his case once a week to the Commandant at Lisbon.

ADJUTANT GENERAL'S OFFICE.

G. O. *Celorico, 20th August*, 1810.

1. THE General Orders of the 17th December, 1810, specifying the ticket to be sent to the General Hospital with sick soldiers, is applicable to detachments as well as regiments.

2. It is extraordinary that the Commander of the Forces should be obliged to remind the Officers of the army in General Orders, of the common practices and forms of the service, and of the standing Military Regulations; as if these Forms and Regulations were not founded on the same principle of utility, and were not particularly necessary in an army on service in a foreign country.

3. The ticket required under the General Orders of this army to be sent with soldiers, is that in use throughout Great Britain, and ordered by His Majesty's Regulations.

4. The King's Regulations, likewise, and the common forms of the service require, that, when an Officer is passing through a town in which there are troops, he should report himself to the Commanding or staff Officer there stationed. All this is neglected to the great inconvenience of the service.

5. The Commander of the Forces will at last find him-

self

self under the necessity of bringing to trial those Officers who shall neglect the performance of the common duties required, not only by the General Orders of this army, but by the King's Regulations and the universal practice of the service at home, as well as abroad.

6. The following men were sent to the Hospital at Coimbra without returns of necessaries:

14th Light Dragoons, Serjeant Lee,

43d Regt. 1st Bn. Isaac Riggs, and Patrick Conolly, from a detachment passing under the command of Captain O'Flaherty, 48d Regiment.

ADJUTANT GENERAL'S OFFICE.

G. O. *Alverca, 22d August,* 1810.

1. AT a General Court Martial, held by virtue of a warrant and in pursuance of an order from His Excellency Lord Viscount Wellington, whereof Major Gen. Lightburne was President, and Captain Goodman Deputy Judge Advocate, was arraigned Private James Jenny of the 27th Regiment, on the following charges, viz.

FIRST CHARGE.

For robbing the Military Chest of a considerable sum of money, when an escort of treasure from Lisbon to the Head Quarters of the army, on or about the month of April last.

SECOND CHARGE.

For deserting at or near Coimbra from the detachment to which he belonged in escorting treasure from Lisbon to Head Quarters on or about the month of April last.

OPINION AND SENTENCE.

The Court having maturely and deliberately weighed and

 con-

considered the evidence adduced in support of the prosecution against the prisoner, Private James Jenny of the 27th Regiment, and what he has offered in his defence, are of opinion he is guilty of the first charge exhibited against him, viz. For robbing the Military Chest of a considerable sum of money when an escort with treasure from Lisbon to the Head Quarters of the army, on or about the month of April last. The Court are further of opinion that the prisoner, Private James Jenny of the 27th Regiment, is guilty of having absented himself from the detachment to which he belonged, in escorting treasure from Lisbon to the Head Quarters on or about the month of April last, (the whole being in breach of the Articles of War) and do by virtue thereof sentence him, the prisoner, James Jenny, Private of the 27th Regiment, to be hanged by the neck till dead, at such time and place as His Excellency the Commander of the Forces may deem fit.

Which sentence has been confirmed by His Excellency the Commander of the Forces.

2. The sentence of the General Court Martial on the prisoner, Private James Jenny, is to be carried into execution on the evening of the 23d instant, in presence of the troops at Guarda, to be paraded for that purpose, under the direction of the Assistant Provost Marshal of the 4th Division.

3. At a General Court Martial, held by virtue of a warrant and in pursuance of an order from His Excellency Lieutenant General Lord Viscount Wellington, whereof Major General Lightburne was President, and Captain Goodman Deputy Judge Advocate, held at Mello, 16th August, 1810, was arraigned Private Bisping of the 1st German Hussars, on the following charges, viz.

for

For deserting on or about the 7th day of August, 1810, when under confinement in the Provost Guard, at St. Jago, for various offences committed by the said Bisping when at or near Castello Bom.

OPINION AND SENTENCE.

The Court having maturely and deliberately weighed and considered the evidence adduced on the prosecution against the prisoner, Private Charles Bisping, and what he has offered in his defence, are of opinion that he is guilty of the charge exhibited against him, (being in breach of the Articles of War) and do by virtue thereof sentence him, the prisoner, Charles Bisping, of the 1st Hussars, to be transported as a felon for seven years, and to be at the expiration of such term of years at the disposal of His Majesty for service as a soldier in any of His Majesty's Regiments at home or abroad for life.

Which judgment has been confirmed by His Excellency the Commander of the Forces.

4. At a General Court Martial, held by virtue of a warrant and in pursuance of an order from His Excellency Lieutenant General Lord Viscount Wellington, whereof Major General Lightburne was President, and Captain Goodman Deputy Judge Advocate, held at Mello, 16th August, 1810, was arraigned Private Thomas Hewitt, of the 2d Battalion 53d Regiment, on the following charges, viz.

FIRST CHARGE.

For repeatedly deserting from his Regiment, particularly on or about the 15th May, 1810.

 SECOND

SECOND CHARGE.

For repeatedly making away with his arms, accoutrements, necessaries, and ammunition.

OPINION AND SENTENCE.

The Court having maturely and deliberately weighed and considered the evidence in support of the prosecution against the prisoner, Private Thomas Hewitt, of the 2d Battalion 53d Regiment, together with what he has offered in his defence, are of opinion that he is guilty of the charges exhibited against him, (being in breach of the Articles of War) and do by virtue thereof sentence him to be transported as a felon for life.

Which sentence has been confirmed by His Excellency the Commander of the Forces."

5. The prisoners, Hewitt and Bisping, are to be sent to Lisbon in irons by the first opportunity.

ADJUTANT GENERAL'S OFFICE.

G. O. *Alverca, 23d August*, 1810.

1. THE General Court Martial of which Major General Lightburne is President, is adjourned till further orders, and the members will return to their duty.

2. Lieutenant Skirvington of the 11th Regiment will place himself under the orders of Marshal Beresford.

G. O.

ADJUTANT GENERAL'S OFFICE

G. O. *Alverca, 24th August*, 1810.

1. AT a General Court Martial held by virtue of a warrant and in pursuance of an order from His Excellency Lieutenant General Lord Viscount Wellington, Commander of the Forces, whereof Major General Lightburne was President, and Captain Goodman Deputy Judge Advocate, held at Mello, 20th August, 1810, was arraigned Serjeant Luttrel of the 16th Light Dragoons, and Serjeant Chandler of the 13th Light Dragoons, on the following charges, viz.

FIRST CHARGE.

For breaking open, at or near Cea, a box of wearing apparel belonging to Colonel Brand of the Coldstream Guards, and stealing thereout various articles of clothes belonging to the said Colonel Brand, on or about the 1st of June, 1810.

SECOND CHARGE.

For having in their possession sundry stolen articles, the property of the said Colonel Brand.

THIRD CHARGE.

For being concerned in selling a pair of boots, belonging to the said Colonel Brand, and for which they received the sum of six dollars, or thereabouts.

OPINION AND SENTENCE.

The Court having maturely and deliberately weighed and

considered the evidence adduced in support of the prosecution against the Prisoner, Serjeant Luttrel of the 16th Light Dragoons, together with what they have brought forward in their defence and the evidence thereon, are of opinion that the Prisoner, Serjeant Luttrel, 16th Light Dragoons, is not guilty of the charge preferred against him; it appearing to the Court that he has satisfactorily accounted for the stockings found in his possession, and do acquit him of the same.

The Court are further of opinion, that the Prisoner, Serjeant Chandler of the 13th Light Dragoons, is guilty of the second part of the first charge exhibited against him, viz. Stealing thereout several articles of clothes belonging to the said Colonel Brand, on or about the 1st June, 1810.

The Court are of opinion the Prisoner is not guilty of the first part of the first charge, viz. For breaking open at or near Cea, a box of wearing apparel belonging to Colonel Brand of the Coldstream Guards, and do acquit him thereof.

The Court are further of opinion that the Prisoner, Serjeant Chandler of the 13th Light Dragoons, is guilty of the second and third charges preferred against him, viz.

2dly. For having in his possession several stolen articles the property of the said Colonel Brand.

3dly. For being concerned in selling a pair of boots belonging to the said Colonel Brand, and for which he received the sum of six dollars, or thereabouts, (the whole being in breach of the Articles of War,) and do by virtue thereof, sentence him the Prisoner, Serjeant Chandler of the 13th Light Dragoons, to be reduced to the rank and pay of a private soldier, and as such private soldier, to

receive

receive a corporal punishment of 1000 lashes at such time and place, and in such manner, as His Excellency the Commander of the Forces may deem fit.

Which sentence has been confirmed by His Excellency the Commander of the Forces.

2. The Prisoner Serjeant Luttrel is to be released forthwith, and is to join his Regiment.

The Prisoner Chandler is to be marched a prisoner to the 13th Light Dragoons; the Commanding Officer of which Regiment will receive further orders respecting him.

3. The Commander of the Forces publishes for general information, the following letter from His Majesty's Minister at Lisbon, and the translation of a paper enclosed, being the proposal for a subscription to raise a sum for the release of several Portuguese captives at Algiers, to which it is the intention of the Commander of the Forces to subscribe 500 dollars.

(Copy)

Lisbon, 9th August, 1810.

My Lord,

In compliance with a request from the Portuguese Government, I have the honor to enclose the copy of a letter I have received from Don M. Forgas, accompanied by a printed proposal to raise the money necessary for the redemption of the Portuguese captives at Algiers, which has been circulated at Lisbon.

If any of the British Officers under your command shall be disposed to contribute towards this object, I suppose you will have the goodness to favor me with the names, and the account of the money collected, that I may

may be enabled to make a proper communication on the subject to the government of this country.

(Signed) CHARLES STEWART.

To the Right Honorable
Lord Viscount Wellington,
&c. &c. &c.

A voluntary and charitable subscription is hereby proposed for the redemption of the Portuguese captives at Algiers.

A convention having been concluded through the powerful mediation of His Britannic Majesty, between the government of the Kingdom of Portugal and the Dey of Algiers, on the 6th July last, by virtue of which an armistice for two years is to take place, and 615 Portuguese who have, for a long time, suffered under a hard captivity, are to be redeemed for the sum of 642,857 Spanish dollars, and three reals equal to reis 514,285,340 Portuguese coin—the Portuguese government, being actually involved in difficult circumstances; and being obliged to make the greatest efforts to maintain, clothe, and pay the large army, which the independence and defence of the nation requires, cannot as they would wish to do, dispose of so large sum, and therefore, convinced that different persons would wish to partake of an action so humane, religious, meritorious, and praiseworthy, have ordered a voluntary subscription to be opened, with the object of completing the above mentioned sum for the redemption of their unfortunate countrymen.

The subscription to be collected and carefully kept by ten honest merchants named for this purpose. In the name of humanity and religion, His Highness the Prince Regent

Regent and the Nation, they exhort all persons to contribute to an act that will bring upon them the blessing of Heaven, the gratitude of the captives, and the love of their country, which will be honoured by leaving this good example to posterity; and will convince the enemy that the Portuguese are not only disposed to defend their independence and liberty, but also are ready to redeem their enslaved brothers.

4. Such officers as chuse to contribute to this charitable purpose, will report their names and the sums they propose to contribute, to the Adjutant General of the division in which they are placed.

ADJUTANT GENERAL'S OFFICE.

G. O. *Alverca, 25th August*, 1810.

1. AT a General Court Martial, held by virtue of a warrant and in pursuance of an order from His Excellency Lord Viscount Wellington, whereof Major General Lightburne was President, and Captain Goodman Deputy Judge Advocate, held at Mello, 21st August, 1810, was arraigned Private William Irwin of the 50th Regiment, on the following charges, viz.

FIRST CHARGE.

For deserting at or near Celerico, on or about the 2d August last.

SECOND CHARGE.

For robbing his master, Major Nappier, 50th Regiment, of

of a sum of money, at or near Celorico, on or about the 2d day of August last.

OPINION AND SENTENCE.

The Court having maturely and deliberately weighed and considered the evidence adduced in support of the prosecution against the prisoner, Private William Irwin of the 50th Regiment, together with what he has offered in his defence, and the evidence thereon, are of opinion, he is guilty of the 1st charge preferred against him, viz.

For deserting at or near Celorico, on or about the 2d August last, (being in breach of the Articles of War) and do by virtue thereof, sentence him to receive a corporal punishment of 1,000 lashes on his bare back, at such time and place as his Excellency the Commander of the Forces may deem fit.

The Court are further of opinion, that the prisoner, Private William Irwin, of the 50th Regiment, is not guilty of the 2d charge preferred against him, viz. For robbing his master, Major Nappier, 50th Regiment, of a sum of money, at or near Celorico, on or about the 2d August last, and do acquit him of the same.

Which judgment and sentence has been confirmed by his Excellency the Commander of the Forces.

ADJUTANT GENERAL'S OFFICE.

G. O. *Alverca, 26th August,* 1810.

1. THE Paymasters of regiments are to go to Pinhancos, to receive from the Paymaster General the balance due on their estimates to the 24th August.

2. Ensign

2. Ensign Lima, 2d battalion 48th Regiment, is attached to the Staff of Lieutenant General Sir Brent Spencer, in the same situation, and to receive the same allowances as when attached to the Staff of Lieutenant General Sir John Sherbrooke.

(Copy)

Horse-Guards, 23d July, 1810.

MY LORD,

3. HAVING had the honor to lay before the King the proceedings of a General Court Martial held at Lisbon on the 19th June, and continued by adjournments till the 21st of the same month, for the trial of Lieutenant Thomas Dunkin of the 4th Dragoons, who was arraigned on the undermentioned charges, viz.

FIRST CHARGE.

For scandalous and infamous conduct unbecoming the character of an Officer and a gentleman, while in command of a detachment of the 4th Dragoons in the Anacreon Transport on the passage from Portsmouth to Lisbon, by making use of highly improper language to, and striking Hospital Mate Daniel Maginn, an Officer under his command, on or about 7th March, 1810. Also in fighting with, and making use of improper language to the said Hospital Mate Maginn, on the deck of the Anacreon Transport, on or about the 21st March last.

SECOND CHARGE.

For scandalous and infamous conduct unbecoming the character of an Officer and a gentleman, by making use of highly improper language to, and fighting with Hospital Mate

Mate James Malony, an Officer under his command, on the deck of the Anacreon Transport, on or about 19th March, 1810. Upon whichcharges the court came to the following decision:

The Court having maturely and deliberately weighed and considered the evidence adduced in support of the prosecution against the prisoner, Lieutenant Thomas Dunkin of the 4th Dragoons, together with what he has alleged in his defence and the evidence thereon, are of opinion that he is guilty of the 1st charge preferred against him, in as far as making use of highly improper language to, and striking Hospital Mate Maginn, an Officer under his command, on or about the 7th of March, 1810, (being in breach of the Articles of War,) and do by virtue thereof sentence him the prisoner, Lieutenant Thomas Dunkin, of the 4th Dragoons, to be suspended from rank and pay for six calendar months; but the Court, in consideration of the grossly insulting language made use of by Hospital Mate Maginn to the prisoner, do acquit him of scandalous and infamous conduct unbecoming the character of an Officer and a gentleman.

The Court are of opinion that the prisoner is not guilty of the second part of the first charge preferred against him, viz. In fighting with, and making use of improper language to the said Hospital Mate Maginn, on the deck of the Anacreon Transport, on or about the 21st March last, and do acquit him thereof.

The Court are further of opinion that the prisoner, Lieutenant Thomas Dunkin, is not guilty of the second charge preferred against him, and do therefore acquit him of the same.

I am to acquaint your Lordship that His Majesty confirms

firms the finding and sentence of the Court; but in consideration of all the circumstances of the prisoner's conduct, as they appear upon the face of the proceedings, His Majesty was pleased to command that it should be intimated to Lieutenant Dunkin, that His Majesty has no further occasion for his services.

Your Lordship will therefore acquaint me with the day upon which His Majesty's pleasure is made known to the prisoner Lieutenant Dunkin, as from that day he will cease to receive pay in His Majesty's service.

(Signed) DAVID DUNDAS,
Commander in Chief.

To Lieut. General the Rt. Hon.
Lord Viscount Wellington,
&c. &c. &c.

ADJUTANT GENERAL'S OFFICE.

G. O. *Alverca, 27th August*, 1810.

1. CAPTAIN Ovens, 2d Battalion 38th Regiment, is to put himself under the orders of Marshal Beresford.

2. At a General Court Martial, held by virtue of a warrant, and in pursuance of an order from His Excellency Lieutenant General Lord Viscount Wellington, whereof Major General Lightburne was President, and Captain Goodman, 48th Regiment, Deputy Judge Advocate, held at Mello, August 18th, 1810, were arraigned Privates David Marsden and Peter Ward, of the 4th Dragoons, on the following charges, viz.

FIRST CHARGE.

For being out of quarters after hours, on or about the night

night of the 11th August last, and attempting to commit a murder on the person of Lorenzo Jose and Maria da Costa, Portuguese inhabitants at or near the village of Marcal du Chaō.

SECOND CHARGE.

For robbing the said Portuguese inhabitants, Lorenzo Jose and Maria da Costa, on or about the night of the 11th August last, at or near the village of Marcal du Chaō.

THIRD CHARGE.

For having in their possession various stolen articles, the property of Antonio Ferrara, Portuguese inhabitants and others, at Marcal du Chaō, on or about the 11th August last.

OPINION AND SENTENCE.

The Court having maturely and deliberately weighed and considered the evidence adduced in support of the prosecution against the prisoners, Privates David Marsden and Peter Ward, of the 4th Dragoons, together with what they have offered in their defence, are of opinion that they are both guilty of the charges exhibited against them, (being in breach of the Articles of War,) and do by virtue thereof sentence them, the prisoners, Privates David Marsden and Peter Ward, of the 4th Dragoons, to be hanged by the neck till dead, at such time and place as His Excellency the Commander of the Forces may deem fit.

Which sentence has been confirmed by His Excellency the Commander of the Forces.

3. The sentence of the General Court Martial upon the prisoners,

prisoners, David Marsden and Peter Ward, of the 4th Dragoons, is to be carried into execution on the evening of Tuesday, the 28th inst. under the direction of the Provost Marshal attached to the Cavalry, and in presence of the troops at Lagiosa, to be paraded for that purpose.

G. O.

Adjutant General's Office.
Alverca, 28th August, 1810.

1. The Officers commanding at the several stations, on the high road by which the Parté goes, or in the neighbourhood of the high road, are to keep a man stationed on the road to receive their letters from Head Quarters, or to deliver those to the Parté which they wish to send to Head Quarters, in order that the Parté may not be delayed as it has been hitherto.

The Parté will, in future, have directions to wait for nobody, and to carry on to Thomar all letters which there may be no one stationed on the road to receive.

2. The General Court Martial, of which Major General Lightburne is President, is dissolved.

3. A General Court Martial to assemble at Thomar, on the 7th of September, for the trial of such prisoners as shall be brought before it.

Major General Leith, President.

Members to be furnished by the 9th and 38th Regiments.

G. O.

Adjutant General's Office.
Celerico, 30th August, 1810.

The Paymasters of Regiments will proceed to Galizes,

to

to receive one half of the amount of their estimates, to the 24th September.

ADJUTANT GENERAL'S OFFICE.

G. O. *Celerico*, 31st *August*, 1810.

CAPTAIN William Gomm, of the 9th Regiment, is appointed a Deputy Assistant in the Quarter Master General's Department, until His Majesty's pleasure is known.

ADJUTANT GENERAL'S OFFICE.

G. O. *Celerico*, 1st *September*, 1810.

1. AT a General Court Martial, held by virtue of a warrant, and in pursuance of an order from His Excellency Lieutenant General Lord Viscount Wellington, K.B. whereof Colonel Saunders, 61st Regiment, was President, and Lieutenant Crompton, 9th Regiment, Acting Deputy Judge Advocate, held at Lisbon, 18th August, 1810, was arraigned Hospital Mate, Augustus Krech, on the following charges, viz.

FIRST CHARGE.

For disobedience of orders on the 26th June last, in refusing to go on board the Sally Transport, for the purpose of attending sick from Figuera to Lisbon.

SECOND CHARGE.

For disrespectful conduct in not answering a second letter of the same date, written to the said Hospital Mate, by Abraham Bolton, Deputy Inspector of Hospitals; and by by which the Sally Transport was obliged to proceed on her voyage without medical assistance.

OPINION AND SENTENCE.

The Court having maturely considered the evidence with respect to the prosecution, as well as that produced in the prisoner's defence, is of opinion that the said Hospital Mate, Augustus Krech, is guilty of the first charge preferred against him, viz.

For disobedience of orders on the 26th June last, in refusing to go on board the Sally Transport for the purpose of attending sick, from Figuera to Lisbon: which being a breach of the Articles of War, and do therefore sentence him, the said Augustus Krech, to be suspended from rank and pay for six calendar months.

With respect to the second charge, viz.

For disrespectful conduct in not answering a second letter of the same date, written to the said Hospital Mate, by Abraham Bolton, Deputy Inspector; and by which the Sally Transport was obliged to proceed on her voyage without medical assistance.

The Court is of opinion that he, the said Hospital Mate, Augustus Krech, is not guilty of shewing any intentional disrespect to Dr. Bolton's letter, as the prisoner, who is a foreigner, does not seem to have understood the orders in the said letter; but thought from the latter expression in it that he was not to take any further notice of it, and therefore sent no answer. The Court do therefore honourably acquit him of the same.

Which decision and sentence have been confirmed by his Excellency the Commander of the Forces.

2. Although the Commander of the Forces is strongly

 impressed

impressed with a sense of the impropriety of the conduct of Mr. Krech, he is induced to remit the punishment to which he has been sentenced, in consequence of the recommendation of the General Court Martial; and he hopes that Mr. Krech will not in future be guilty of similar disobedience of Orders.

Mr. Krech is to be released from his arrest, and is to return to his duty.

ADJUTANT GENERAL'S OFFICE.

G. O. *Gouvea, 5th September,* 1810.

THE Rev. Thomas Williams is placed on the strength of the Army, as Chaplain to the Forces, from 25th July.

ADJUTANT GENERAL'S OFFICE.

G. O. *Gouvea, 8th September,* 1810.

(Copy.) *St. Martinho, 7th September,* 1810.

SIR,

1. I BEG leave to inform you that the Paymaster of this Battalion having left Guarda on the 27th ultimo, in consequence of his General Orders of the preceding day, has not since made his appearance at the quarter of the Regiment. Much inconvenience having been felt from the absence of Mr. Clarke, I have taken every step I could to find him out; but after ascertaining that he received balances from the Paymaster General on the

the 30th ultimo, I have not been able to discover what has become of him since that day.

(Signed) C. A. HARCOURT,
Commanding 1st Battalion 40th Regiment.

To Major General
The Honourable Lowry Cole,
&c. &c. &c.

Officers commanding Regiments are to report if the Paymaster of the 40th Regiment is at the quarters of any of the Regiments of the Army.

2. His Majesty has been pleased to approve of the undermentioned Officers being continued on the Staff of the Army in Portugal, from 25th July, 1810, viz.

Major-General Alexander Campbell,
——————— Richard Stewart,
——————— The Hon. Charles Stewart,
——————— Sigismond Baron Low,
——————— Alan Cameron,
——————— Henry Fane,
——————— George Anson.

3. Lieutenants Boyce and Beaver, of the 43d Regiment, will proceed to England to join the 2d Battalion, to which they belong.

Captains Sowerby and Lascelles, Coldstream Guards, will proceed to England to join the 2d Battalion to which they belong.

Memorandum.—Divine Service will be performed to-morrow morning at 7 o'clock, for the 4th and Light Divisions, in the open ground on this side Penhances, where they are to assemble.

 ADJUTANT

ADJUTANT GENERAL'S OFFICE.

G. O. *Gouvea, 10th September,* 1810.

A BOARD of Enquiry, consisting of an Officer of the Quarter Master General's Department, one Officer of the Commissariat Department, and a Subaltern of the Light Division, to assemble to-morrow morning at 10 o'clock, in Captain Kelly's quarters, to enquire into the circumstances of a murder said to be committed by five Spaniards now in the Provost Guard, on the body of a Portuguese peasant.

ADJUTANT GENERAL'S OFFICE.

G. O. *Gouvea, 11th September,* 1810.

(Copy.) *Isla de Leon, August 31st,* 1810.

MY LORD,

1. As there has been a delay in sending the returns of this Division, I wish to inform your Lordship of the cause of the disappointment.

On the 15th inst. the following official memorandum was sent to the 79th and 88th Regiments.

The 79th and 88th Regiments to furnish the Assistant Adjutant General in the course of the day with the Monthly Returns, for the months of April and May, according to the new printed form which has been circulated.

(Signed) J. MACDONALD.
Assistant Adjutant General.

The 79th complied with the order immediately; but the 88th, though the Returns were repeatedly called for, through

through the Brigade Major in the course of that day, embarked and sailed without sending any Returns or explanation whatever concerning them.

In consequence, an application made by the Adjutant General of the Forces, cannot be complied with.

(Signed) THOMAS GRAHAM,
Lieutenant General.

Lieutenant General
Lord Viscount Wellington, K. B.
&c. &c. &c.

2. The Officer commanding the 2d Battalion 88th Regiment will account forthwith for the neglect and disobedience of orders reported in the foregoing letter from Lieutenant General Graham.

3. The Rev. George Jenkins, Chaplain to the Forces from 25th July, having arrived at the Head Quarters of the Army, is to be attached to the 4th Division, till further orders.

4. Captain Donnaghoe, 44th Regiment, and Lieutenant Mar, 87th Regiment, are to place themselves under the Orders of Marshal Beresford.

ADJUTANT GENERAL'S OFFICE.

G. O. *Gouvea, 12th September, 1810.*

1. LIEUTENANT Simon Newport is appointed to act as Adjutant to the 2d Battalion 39th Regiment, till his Majesty's pleasure is known.

2. The 79th Regiment is to be part of Major General Cameron's Brigade.

3. The 1st Battalion Royal Fusileers and 61st Regi-

ment are to form a Brigade, and this Brigade is to be in the 1st Division until further orders.

4. The 2d Battalion 83d Regiment is to be posted in Major General Lightburne's Brigade.

5. A General Court Martial will assemble at Moita, on the 14th inst. for the trial of such prisoners as may be brought before it.

President, Colonel the Honourable Edward Stopford; Acting Deputy Judge Advocate Captain Andrews, 60th Regt. The members to be furnished by the 1st Division.

6. A General Court Martial to assemble on the 14th, at Mello.

President, Major General Slade.

The Members to be furnished by the Cavalry Division.

ADJUTANT GENERAL'S OFFICE.
A. G. O. *Gouvea, 12th September,* 1810.

1. OFFICERS are appointed to the Staff at Cadiz as follows, till His Majesty's pleasure is known.

Colonel Wheatly, 2d Battalion 1st Guards, to command a Brigade, vice Santay . 11Aug.1810

Captain Clutterbuck, 2d Battalion 1st Guards, to be Major of Brigade, vice Douglass, who has joined his Regiment 17do.

Captain Mallet, 2d Battalion 30th Regiment, Town Major, Cadiz, and Deputy Assistant Quarter Master General, vice Campbell, who has joined his Regiment 29July

Captain Chalmers, 52d Regiment, Brigade Major, vice Tryon, removed to Staff in Portugal . . . . 18Aug.

Lieutenant

Lieutenant Russell, 2d Battalion 44th Regiment, Assistant Engineer, vice Ford, who has joined his Regiment . . . . 10 Aug. 1810

Lieutenant Bryant, 2d Battalion 44th Regiment, Deputy Adjutant Quarter Master General, vice Walker, who has joined his Regiment . . . . 18 do.

Lieutenant Erskine, 94th Regiment, Assistant Engineer, vice Cameron, who has joined his Regiment . . . . do.

2. Brigade Major Tryon is appointed to the Brigade of Infantry consisting of the 7th or Fusileers, and 61st Regiment.

ADJUTANT GENERAL'S OFFICE,
G. O. *Gouvea, 13th September,* 1810.

1. AT a General Court Martial, held by virtue of a warrant and in pursuance of an order from his Excellency Lieutenant General Lord Viscount Wellington, K. B. whereof Major General Leith was President, and Captain Goodman Deputy Judge Advocate, held at Thomar, 7th September, 1810, was arraigned Captain John Wilson, 3d Battalion Royals, on the following charge, viz.

For disrespectful expressions, and conduct unbecoming the character of an Officer and a gentleman, and highly subversive of Military Discipline, at the evening parade of the 3d Battalion Royals, on the 19th day of June, 1810.

In making use of the following expressions or words to that effect, addressed to his Commanding Officer, Lieutenant Colonel Barnes, before the Captains and Officers commanding

commanding Companies, called forward to receive orders in front of the Battalion, viz. "That he Lieutenant Colonel Barnes, also the Quarter-Master, had deceived him;" and for refusing to withdraw the abovementioned disrespectful expressions, when immediately offered to be released from arrest, on condition of his doing so.

OPINION AND SENTENCE.

The Court having maturely and deliberately weighed and considered the Evidence adduced in support of the prosecution against the Prisoner, Captain John Wilson, 3d Battalion Royals, as well as what he has brought forward in his defence, and the Evidence thereon, are of opinion that he is guilty of a part of the 1st part of the charge exhibited against him, viz.

For disrespectful expressions, unbecoming the character of an Officer, and subversive of military discipline, at the evening parade of the 3d Battalion Royals, on the 19th day of June, 1810.

In making use of the following expressions or words to that effect, addressed to his Commanding Officer Lieutenant Colonel Barnes, before the Captains and Officers commanding Companies, called forward to receive orders in front of the Battalion, viz.

That he Lieutenant Colonel Barnes, also the Quarter Master, had deceived him.

The Court are also of opinions that the prisoner Captain John Wilson, 3d Battalion Royals, is guilty of the latter part of the charge exhibited against him, viz.

For refusing to withdraw the abovementioned disrespectful expressions, when immediately offered to be released from arrest on condition of his doing so; being in breach of of the Articles of War, and do by virtue thereof sentence him the Prisoner, Captain John Wilson, of 3d Battalion, Royals, to be publicly reprimanded.

The Court are of opinion that the Prisoner, Captain John Wilson, of 3d Battalion, Royals, is not guilty of conduct unbecoming the character of a gentleman, and do therefore honourably acquit him of the same.

Which sentence has been confirmed by His Excellency the Commander of the Forces.

2. The Commander of the Forces laments that Captain Wilson should have thought proper to defer till he was brought to trial, to explain the disrespectful expressions, which he made use of to his Commanding Officer, notwithstanding the repeated offers made to him by his Commanding Officer to receive such explanation.

The Officers of the Army should recollect that it is not only no degradation, but it is meritorious for him that is in the wrong to acknowledge and atone for his error, and that the momentary humiliation which any man may feel, upon making such an acknowledgment, is more than atoned for by the subsequent satisfaction which it affords him, and by avoiding a trial and conviction of conduct unbecoming an Officer.

The Commander of the Forces requests that Major General Leith will have this Order read to Captain Wilson, in front of the Royals paraded for that purpose, as the reprimand for his conduct.

Captain Wilson is to be released from his arrest.

G. O.

ADJUTANT GENERAL'S OFFICE.

G. O. *Gouvea, 14th September, 1810.*

(Copy.) WAR OFFICE.
20th August, 1810.

MY LORD,

I HAVE the honour to acquaint your Lordship that His Majesty has been pleased to direct, that the same allowances shall be made to the widows and children of soldiers dying abroad, and sent home in consequence thereof, as are granted to the wives and children of soldiers embarking for foreign service.

To entitle persons to the allowances in question, it will be necessary that they should produce certificates from the Commanding Officers of the Corps, to which their husbands or fathers "as the case may be," died abroad, and that they are therefore sent home.

(Signed) PALMERSTON.

To Lieutenant General
Lord Viscount Wellington,
&c. &c. &c.

2. Captain Yuhlke of the 60th Regiment will place himself under the orders of Marshal Beresford.

Memorandum.—Regiments and Corps will immediately send in to the Adjutant General's Office, Returns of women and children actually present in this country.

A. G. O.

ADJUTANT GENERAL'S OFFICE.

A. G. O. Gouvea, 14th September, 1810.

No. 2 of the General Orders of the 12th instant, is suspended until further orders.

ADJUTANT GENERAL'S OFFICE.

G. O. Cea, 17th September, 1810.

1. THE Paymasters of Regiments in the 1st, 3d, and 4th Divisions of Infantry, will attend at the Pay Master General's as soon as possible at Ponte de Marcella, or at Foz d'Arouce to receive the balance due on their estimates to the 24th instant.

2. Captain Hill, of the Royal Light Infantry Rangers, and Lieutenant Haddock, 87th Regiment, are to place themselves under the orders of Marshal Beresford.

ADJUTANT GENERAL'S OFFICE.

G. O. Cortico, 18th September, 1810.

THE several Corps of the Army will immediately transmit to the Quarter Master General's Office, Returns for 165 days Forage Money, for the period commencing on the 17th instant, and ending on the 28th February, 1811.

Commanding Officers are referred to the printed Regulations, respecting Bat and Forage Money allowances, dated May, 1809, and inserted in the General Orders of the

the 1st September of the same year, as also the Circular Letter of the Commander in Chief, dated Horse Guards, 17th July, 1809, and inserted in the General Orders of 23d September, 1809.

ADJUTANT GENERAL'S OFFICE.

P. O. *Cortico, 18th September,* 1810.

THE sick of the Light Division and Cavalry, are still to be sent to Riva, those of the 3d, 4th, and 1st Divisions are to remain under the care of the Surgeons of their Divisions, until a place is fixed on for the boats to assemble in the rear of Riva, to which they will hereafter be sent.

ADJUTANT GENERAL'S OFFICE.

G. O. *Cortico, 19th September,* 1810.

COLONEL The Hon. Edward Pakenham will proceed to Coimbra, to take upon him the command of the Brigade, consisting of the 7th and 79th Regiments.

Brigade Major Tryon is attached to this Brigade, till further orders.

ADJUTANT GENERAL'S OFFICE.

A. G. O. *Cortico, 19th September,* 1810.

THE following appointments on the Staff, at Cadiz, have taken place.

Major-General Ferguson, 25th May, 1810, Aid de Camp.
Captain G. Elliot, 1st Guards, ... Do. Do.
Extra A. D. C. Lieut. Synge, 10th Lt. Dragoons Do. Do.

Brigade

Brigade Major, Captain Machell, 30th Regiment, 9th July, 1810.

Physician to the Forces, John Plenderleath, M. D. 15th May, 1810.

Surgeons to the Forces.	John Rice, 15th May, 1810. Victor Sugal. Edward Doughty, 15th May, 1810.

Hospital Mates.	Daniel Owen Davis,	15th May,	1810.
	John Pendergast . .	Do.	Do.
	Henry Tate	Do.	Do.
	Samuel Coulthard .	Do.	Do.
	Nathaniel Rube . .	Do.	Do.
	Thomas M'Cready .	Do.	Do.
	Richard Davis . .	Do.	Do.

ADJUTANT GENERAL'S OFFICE,

G. O. *Lovao, 20th September*, 1810.

1. HIS Majesty has been pleased to appoint the undermentioned officers on the Staff of the Army in Portugal.

Major General The Honourable William Lumley, 6th August, 1810.

Colonel Hay of the Royals, as a Brigadier General, 6th August, 1810.

2. Major General C. Tilson has resigned his situation on the Staff of the army in Portugal, from 27th July, in consequence of ill health.

3. The following Medical Officers have been appointed by His Majesty, to the Staff of the Army in Portugal.

Alexander M'Dougal . .	Staff Surgeons joined from Prisoners of War.
Summers Higgins . .	

William

William Williams . . .	Hospital Mates.
William Roberts . . .	
James M'Leod . . .	
James Brady	
Richard Lloyd	
Patrick Henry Levin . .	
John M'Nullen . . .	

Memorandum.—Lieutenant White 13th Light Dragoons, being reported fit for duty, is to join his Regiment forthwith.

ADJUTANT GENERAL'S OFFICE.
P. O. *Lovao, 20th September,* 1810.

ANY sick of the 3d and 4th Divisions on the left bank of the Mondego, are to be sent by the Staff Surgeons to Lorido.

Those Divisions or Corps, that are on the right bank, are to send their sick to Pena Cova.

Staff Surgeons will be sent to Lorido and Pena Cova, to receive them.

N. B. Lorido is on the left bank of the Mondego, a quarter of a league below Pena Cova, the road to it from Ponte de Marcella, is through Cray de Balterra.

ADJUTANT GENERAL'S OFFICE,
P. O. *Busaco, 22d September,* 1810.

THE sick of the 3d Division, and General Leith's corps, will find boats at Pena Cova, to transport them to Coimbra.

Those

Those of the 4th Division, Light Division, and Cavalry, must be forwarded to Botaõ or Mealhada, at each of which places, a depot of cars has been ordered to relieve the divisional cars, and transport the men to Coimbra. The divisional cars will thus return to their divisions.

The sick of the 1st Division must be sent from Mealhada, on the cars with that division to Coimbra, which may then return to Mealhada.

The sick will carry two days provisions, ready cooked, with them.

ADJUTANT GENERAL'S OFFICE.
G. O. *Busaco, 24th September,* 1810.

1. LIEUTENANT Baron Osten, 16th Light Dragoons, is appointed an Extra Aide de Camp, to Lieutenant General Sir Stapleton Cotton.

Memorandum.—Heads of departments will send in to the Adjutant General's Office on the 25th instant, or as soon after as possible, Nominal Returns of the Officers at present serving in their respective departments, specifying the Regiments to which they belong, and the names of the places in which they are stationed.

The Assistant Adjutant Generals attached to divisions, will send in to the Adjutant General's Office on the 25th instant, or as soon after as possible, Nominal Returns of the Generals and other Staff Officers, at present serving in the respective divisions, specifying the nature of their appointments, regiments and stations, and to note at the bottom any alterations which have taken place, during the preceding month.

 Colonel

Colonel Darrock, Assistant Adjutant General, will likewise send in a return of the Generals and Staff Officers at Lisbon.

Regiments and corps will send in with their Monthly Returns for the 25th of September, Quarterly Returns of Officers who have been absent without leave, for any period, during the preceding three months.

Adjutant General's Office.

G. O. Coimbra, 30th September, 1810.

1. The Commander of the Forces returns his thanks to the General and other Officers and soldiers of the Army, for their conduct during the whole time they occupied the position of Busaco, and in the action with the enemy on the 27th instant.

He witnessed several instances of intrepidity in the officers and troops, and others have been reported to him by the general officers, of which he will not fail to report his sense to His Majesty, and to the government of His Royal Highness the Prince Regent of Portugal.

Every friend to his country and to the liberties of the world and the whole British Army must have observed with the greatest satisfaction the gallantry and steadiness of the Portuguese troops during these days, and that they equally with their brother soldiers in his Majesty's service, have deserved and obtained the approbation of Marshal Beresford, and of the Commander of the Forces.

Although the designs manifested by the enemy's movements, induced the Commander of the Forces to withdraw the Army from their position, which it was not in the power

power of the enemy to force. He hopes to be enabled by the discipline and determined bravery of the officers and troops, to frustrate all his designs, and to save this country, " In which the British Army has been so well treated," from the degrading yoke which is prepared for it.

2. At a general Court Martial held by virtue of a warrant and in pursuance of an order from his Excellency Lieutenant General Lord Viscount Wellington, K. B. held at Celerico, on the 2d day of April, 1810; of which Brigadier General Alexander Campbell was President, and Captain Goodman, 48th Regiment, Deputy Judge Advocate, were arraigned Privates Thomas Horsley, Joseph Norman, Edward Perrot, and Drummer Joseph Freeman of the 45th Regiment, on the following charge, viz. For stopping on the highway, assaulting, and robbing, some Portuguese inhabitant or inhabitants, on or about the 12th March, 1810, at or near the bridge of St. Euphemia.

To which charge the prisoners pleaded not guilty.

OPINION AND SENTENCE.

The Court, having maturely weighed and considered the evidence adduced in support of the prosecution against the prisoners, Privates Thomas Horsley, Joseph Norman, Edward Perrot, and Drummer Joseph Freeman of the 45th Regiment, together with what they have offered in their defence, are of opinion that they are guilty of the charge preferred against them, viz.

For stopping on the highway, assaulting, and robbing some Portuguese inhabitant or inhabitants, on or about the 12th of March, 1810, at or near the bridge of St. Euphemia;

 Being

Being in breach of the Articles of War, and do by virtue thereof sentence them,* the Prisoners, Privates Thomas Horsley, Joseph Norman, Edward Perrot, and Drummer Joseph Freeman, of the 45th Regiment, to be hung by the neck till dead, at such time and place as His Excellency the Commander of the Forces may deem fit.

Which sentence has been confirmed by His Excellency the Commander of the Forces.

3. Although the Commander of the Forces has long determined that he will not pardon men guilty of crimes of which these Prisoners have been convicted, he is induced to pardon these men in consequence of the gallantry displayed by the 45th Regiment on the 27th inst.

He trusts that this pardon will make a due impression upon the Prisoners, and that by their future regular and good conduct, they will endeavour to emulate their comrades, who have by their bravery saved them from a disgraceful end.

4. Major General the Hon. William Lumley and Brigadier General Hay, having joined the army, the former is appointed to command the Brigade of Infantry heretofore commanded by the late Brigadier General Crawford, the latter to the Brigade of Infantry commanded by Lieutenant Colonel Barnes.

The appointment of Lieutenant Colonel Barnes to command a Brigade is discontinued from this day.

ADJUTANT GENERAL'S OFFICE.

G. O. *Leyria, 3d October*, 1810.

1. THE Commanding Officers, of the 3d Battalion Royals, 1st Battalion 9th Regiment, 2d Battalion 38th Regiment,

giment, are referred particularly to the General Orders of the 9th May, 1809.

There are more stragglers from these three regiments, than from all the others of the British Army taken together, which must be occasioned either by the neglect of the Officers, or by the soldiers being unable to keep up with the march.

In either case, these regiments are unfit to do duty with the army; and if the Commander of the Forces should observe any more of this straggling on the march, he will send the regiments into garrison, and report their conduct especially to His Majesty.

2. The Commander of the Forces requests, that Major General Lieth will communicate these Orders to the Portuguese troops in his division, of whom, particularly the Lusitanian Legion, there is as much reason to complain, as of the British brigade.

He also requests to have a Return this day of the number of men missing from each regiment, British and Portuguese, in the division, on each day's march, since the 1st instant inclusive.

3. General Officers commanding divisions are requested to direct the Provost Marshal attached to their division, to punish any man who may be found straggling from the regiment and division to which he belongs.

4. General Officers commanding divisions are requested to direct that there may be an inspection of the soldiers' packs, both British and Portuguese, this day after the march, and every thing, not strictly regimental necessaries, is to be taken from them and burnt, and those who have these articles are to be punished, as they have certainly procured them by plunder.

 Major

Major General Picton is requested not to allow the troops of his division to enter any town unless necessarily obliged to pass through it, until further orders.

Memorandum.—Divisions and brigades, requiring ammunition, will apply to Lieutenant Colonel Robe, who is with Major General Leith's corps.

ADJUTANT GENERAL'S OFFICE.

A. G. O. *Leyria, 3d October,* 1810.

THE Paymasters of regiments will apply to the Paymaster General at Rio Major, to receive the balances on their estimates, to the 24th October.

ADJUTANT GENERAL'S OFFICE.

A. G. O. *Leyria, 3d October,* 1810.

THE Commander of the Forces is concerned to have been under the necessity of carrying into execution the determination which he has so long announced, of directing the immediate execution of any soldiers caught plundering; and that a British and Portuguese soldier have consequently been hanged this day for plundering in the town of Leyria, where they were contrary to order, and for this criminal purpose.

He trusts that this example will deter others from those disgraceful practices in future; and the troops may depend upon it that no instance of the kind will be passed over.

They are well fed and taken care of, and there is no excuse

cuse for plunder, which could not be admitted on any account.

Once more, the Commander of the Forces calls upon the Commanding Officers of regiments to oblige their men to march in a regular manner with their companies.

ADJUTANT GENERAL'S OFFICE,
Leyria, 4th October, 1810.

G. O.

1. THE Commander of the Forces publishes the following report of men absent from the 3d Battalion Royals, 1st Battalion 9th, and 2d Battalion 38th Regiments, and from the Lusitanian Legion.

He desires that an Officer of each regiment may be sent back along the road as far as the advanced guard, to find the men missing; and the Officers commanding the the above regiments will report their arrival.

2. Report of men missing from the different regiments composing Major General Leith's corps, on the 3d October, 1810:

	Rank and File.
3d Battalion, Royals, . .	20
1st do. . . . 9th Reg. . .	5
2d do. . . . 38th Reg. .	11

	Drummer.	Rank and File.
Lusitanian Legion .	1	50

No return as yet from the other Portuguese regiments.

3. The Commander of the Forces trusts that, by the attention of the Officers commanding regiments, this disgraceful circumstance will not occur again.

G. O.

ADJUTANT GENERAL'S OFFICE,
G. O. *Alcobaça, 5th October*, 1810.

1. THE Commander of the Forces announces to the army that thirty of the stragglers, who are absent from their regiments, of which ten are British soldiers, were taken yesterday by the enemy in villages near the road on which the army marched three or four days before, that is on the 1st and 2d instant.

This misfortune would be a subject of regret to the Commander of the Forces under any circumstances, but it is particularly so, as it has been occasioned by the irregularity of the soldiers themselves, and by the neglect of their Officers to attend to the orders repeatedly issued upon this subject.

2. As the divisions of Infantry will pass through Rio Major, three spring waggons will be attached to each, to be under the direction of the Staff Surgeon.

The Staff Surgeons are held responsible that nothing is put into these spring waggons excepting sick soldiers, or their packs or arms.

The Commander of the Forces requests the General Officers commanding divisions, will report to him if they should observe any deviation from this order.

The medical panniers or other medical stores are positively not to be carried in them.

3. Major the Honourable H. Pakenham is appointed an Assistant Adjutant General from the 1st inst. until His Majesty's pleasure is known.

4. His Majesty has been pleased to appoint Major General Sir William Erskine on the staff of the army in Portugal, from the 8th August, 1810.

Captain

Captain Wemyss, 6th Garrison Battalion, is appointed Aide de Camp, and Captain M'Donald, 45th Regiment, extra Aide de Camp to Major General Sir William Erskine, from the date of the Major General's appointment.

ADJUTANT GENERAL'S OFFICE.

G. O. *Rio Major, 6th October*, 1810.

1. THE Regiments are to be arranged in brigades and divisions as follows, until further orders.

2. The 50th, 71st, and 92d Regiments are to form a brigade under the command of Major General Sir William Erskine, and to be in the 1st Division.

3. The 94th are to be in a brigade with the 2d Battalion 5th, and 2d Battalion 83d, under the command of the senior Officer, until further orders. This Brigade is to continue in the 3d Division.

4. The 79th are to be in Major General Cameron's Brigade, and in the 1st Division.

5. The 1st Battalion Fusileers, and 61st, and the Brunswick Infantry are to be in a brigade together under the command of the Honourable Colonel Pakenham, and to be in the 4th Division.

6. The 5th Division of Infantry is to be commanded by Major General Leith, and is to consist of Brigadier General Hay's Brigade, and of a brigade of British Infantry, composed of the 1st Battalion 4th, 2d Battalion 30th, and 2d Battalion 44th, under the command of the senior Officer until further orders; and of Brigadier General Spry's Brigade, of Portuguese Infantry.

7. The 6th Division of Infantry is to be commanded by

by Major General A. Campbell, and is to consist of Major General A. Campbell's Brigade of British Infantry, and Baron Eben's Brigade of Portuguese Infantry.

8. Colonel Pakenham's Brigade, Major General Campbell's Brigade, and Baron Eben's Brigade are to continue with the several divisions with which they are now marching, till opportunity will offer of forming the divisions.

In the mean time, the Commissary General will make the arrangements for placing a Commissariat Staff with Sir William Erskine's Brigade, and the brigade of British Infantry to be added to the 5th Division.

9. Captain Achmuty is to act as a Deputy Assistant Adjutant General till His Majesty's pleasure is known, and is to do duty with the 6th Division of Infantry when it will be formed.

10. The Quarter Master General will make arrangements for sending an Officer of the Quarter Master General's Department with the 6th Division.

ADJUTANT GENERAL'S OFFICE.

G. O. *Alenquer, 7th October,* 1810.

1. THE Commanding Officer of Artillery will attach to the British troops, in the 5th and 6th Divisions of Infantry, the same proportion of musquet-ammunition and flints for their numbers as is attached to the other divisions, and will make a requisition upon the Commissary General for mules to carry it.

G. O.

ADJUTANT GENERAL'S OFFICE,

G. O. *Alenquer, 8th October,* 1810.

1. MAJOR General Houghton is appointed to command Major General R. Stewart's Brigade of Infantry in the 2d Division, during the indisposition of Major General R. Stewart.

2. The Commander of the Forces requests that now that the troops will have arrived in their positions, the General Officers commanding divisions will order them to clean themselves, as he proposes to look at each division in the course of a day or two.

Memorandum.—Lieutenant Colonel the Honourable F. Ponsonby, Assistant Adjutant General is attached to the troops under the orders of Major General Fane till further orders.

Captain George Napier, of the 52d Regiment, has the Commander of the Forces leave of absence for two months to Lisbon, for the recovery of health.

ADJUTANT GENERAL'S OFFICE.

G. O. *Arruda, 9th October,* 1810.

1. DEPUTY Assistant Commissary General Carey is appointed to the brigade commanded by Major General Sir William Erskine in the 1st Division.

2. Deputy Assistant Commissary General St. Remy is appointed to the brigade, consisting of the 1st Battalion 4th, 2d Battalion 30th, and 2d Battalion 44th Regiments in the 5th Division.

3. Captain George Hay, 3d Battalion Royals, is appointed

pointed Aide de Camp to Brigadier General Hay, from the date of the Brigadier General's appointment to the Staff of the Army in Portugal.

4. Staff Surgeon Irwin is attached to the 6th Division of Infantry.

5. The Returns of the Army cannot be made up unless Officers commanding regiments send in their returns according to Genreal Orders.

The following returns are now wanting, and the Assistant Adjutant Generals of division will immediately collect and forward them to the Adjutant General's Office.

Disembarkation Returns.

50th Regiment 1st Battalion,
94th do. do.
Light Infantry Duke of Brunswick's Corps,
Detachment 3d Battalion 95th Regiment.

Monthly Returns for the 25th September, 1810.

13th Light Dragoons,
16th do. do.
1st Hussars, King's German Legion,
Royal Engineers,
Royal Waggon Train,
General Staff of the 2d Division of Infantry,
General Staff of the 4th Division of Infantry,
General Staff of the Cavalry Division,
Commissary General's Department,
Paymaster General's Department,
Commissary of Accounts do.
Chaplains.

Quarterly

Quarterly Returns of absent Officers without Leave.

1st or Royal Dragoons,
13th Light do.
14th do. do.
16th do. do.
1st Hussars King's German Legion,
5th Regiment, 2d Battalion,
45th do. 1st do.
74th do.
83d do. 2d do.
88th do. 1st do.
95th do. 1st do.

States for the 1st October, 1810.

Cavalry Division.
1st Division of Infantry, previous to the new arrangement.
1st Company 2d Battalion 95th Regiment,
Detachment 3d do. 95th do.
Duke of Brunswick's Corps,
Royal Waggon Train,
50th Regiment 1st Battalion,
Detachment 1st Battalion 71st Regiment.

ADJUTANT GENERAL'S OFFICE.
G. O. *Arruda*, 10*th October*, 1810.

1. CAPTAIN Foljambe, of the 20th Regiment, is appointed Aide de Camp to Major General the Honourable William Lumley from the date of the Major General's appointment to the staff in Portugal.

2. Major

2. Major General the Honourable C. Colville is appointed by His Majesty to the Staff of the Army in Portugal from 1st September, and is to command the Brigade of Infantry in the 3d Division, consisting of the 2d Battalion 5th, 2d Battalion 83d and 94th Regiments.

3. Captain Cotton, of the Fusileers, is to act as Brigade Major to the Brigade of British Infantry, in the 6th Division, until further orders.

4. Fernando Antonio Machardo is appointed a Cornet in the corps of Guides, with pay and allowances of a Cornet of Cavalry, from 16th September, 1810.

ADJUTANT GENERAL'S OFFICE.

A. G. O. *Arruda, 10th October,* 1810.

THE sick of the several divisions are to be sent in the first instance from the present Head Quarters of these divisions as follows:

From 3d Division at Torres Vedras - - to Mafra.

From the 5th Division at Enexera de los Cavalleros—from the 6th Division at Ribaldeira - - - - - - - to Montachique

From the 4th Division at Doïs Portes; the 1st Division at Sobral; and the Light Division to Bucellas.

From the 2d Division, &c. under Lieutenant General Hill at Alhandra - - - by water to to Lisbon, and if that cannot be done to Saccavem by land.

The Commissary General will provide for the conveyance of the sick from the above points to Lisbon.

The Cavalry under Lieutenant General Sir Stapleton Cotton

Cotton will send their sick from Mafra; and the Cavalry under Major General Fane will send their's direct from Loures to Lisbon.

G. O.

ADJUTANT GENERAL'S OFFICE.
Santa Quintina, 11*th October*, 1810.

OFFICERS are requested when they send any report, to take particular care to date the hours they dispatch it, the day and place from which they send it.

A. G. O.

ADJUTANT GENERAL'S OFFICE.
Santa Quintina, 11*th October*, 1810.

1. BRIGADE Major Machell is appointed Brigade Major to the Brigade of Infantry, consisting of the 1st Battalion 4th, 2d Battalion 30th, and 2d Battalion 44th Regiments from the 1st instant.

2. Captain M'Donald, 45th Regiment, is appointed Brigade Major to the Brigade of Infantry, consisting of 50th, 71st, and 92d Regiments from the 1st instant.

3. The Commander of the Forces publishes in General Orders the names of Officers ordered by the Commandant at Lisbon to march with detachments of sick from Lisbon, but who did not obey the order.

4. The Officers commanding the Regiments to which they belong, are desired to call upon them to account for their misconduct.

Regiments.

31st—Quarter Master M'Intosh not present when the party marched.

83d—

Regiments.

83d—Lieutenant Irwin not present when the party marched.

88th—	Captain M'Dougall	do.	do.
—	Captain Hogan	do.	do.
—	Lieutenant Dabin	do.	do.
—	Lieutenant Walker	do.	do.
—	Ensign Hilliard	do.	do.
—	Ensign Rutherford	do.	do.

Memorandum.—The spring waggons that have been unable, from the badness of the roads, to join the 1st, 4th, and Light Divisions, are ordered to remain at Enexara de los Cavallieros until further orders.

ADJUTANT GENERAL'S OFFICE,

G. O. *Rinho, near Sobral, 13th October,* 1810.

WHEN any Officer is desirous of communicating a message to the Commander of the Forces, it is only necessary to send it to the nearest telegraph and to request the Officer of the navy at that telegraph to communicate it to the Sobral station: in the same manner messages may be communicated to any other station.

ADJUTANT GENERAL'S OFFICE.

G. O. *Rinho, 14th October,* 1810.

1. ENSIGN Desbrowe, 1st Regiment of Guards, is appointed extra Aide de Camp to Major General the Hon. William Stewart from the 1st instant.

2. Serjeant

2. Serjeant Frosdick, 11th Regiment, is appointed an Assistant Provost Marshal from the 10th instant, and is to do duty in the 6th Division.

3. The following are the only regiments of the army, whose returns of Field Equipments for the 1st instant, have reached the Quarter Master General.

43d Regiment	———	94th Regiment.
52d Do.	———	45th Do.
95th Do.	———	3 Companies 5th Bat. 60th
5th Do.	———	74th.
83d Do.	———	88th 1st Battalion.

ADJUTANT GENERAL'S OFFICE.

A. G. O. *Rinho, 14th October*, 1810.

1. CAPTAIN Leggatt, 50th Regiment, is appointed to act as an Extra Aide de Camp, to Major General The Honourable William Lumley, from the 14th instant.

2. Baron Drechsel, Brigade Major to the brigade of the K. G. Legion, having arrived from England, is to succeed Captain Backmeister, who has been acting as such, and who will join his battalion.

ADJUTANT GENERAL'S OFFICE.

G. O. *Enaxara de los Cavalleros, 15th October*, 1810.

1. CAPTAIN Craig of the 30th Regiment, is appointed a Deputy Assistant Adjutant General until his Majesty's pleasure is known, from the 14th instant, and is attached to the 4th Division of Infantry, vice Captain Cooke, Deputy

Assistant Adjutant General, who will do duty with the 1st Division.

2. General Officers who have detained Orderly Dragoons without the express permission of the Commander of the Forces, and who are not entitled to them, are desired to send them forthwith to Mafra, to join the Head Quarters of their regiment.

ADJUTANT GENERAL'S OFFICE.

G. O. *Enexara de los Cavalleros, 16th October*, 1810.

1. MAJOR GENERAL the Honourable Charles Colville's appointment to the Staff of the Army in Portugal, is from the 25th of August, instead of the 1st September, as stated in General Orders of the 10th instant.

2. Lieutenant Brawn, Captain Retberg's brigade, Royal German Artillery, is to place himself under the orders of Marshal Beresford.

3. Lieutenant Oliveira of the Portuguese service is attached to the division under the orders of Major General Leith, from 1st September. He will receive pay and allowances as Ensign, and be allowed to draw forage for a horse, agreeable to No. 12. of the General Orders of the 6th May, 1809.

ADJUTANT GENERAL'S OFFICE.

G. O. *Pero Negro, 17th October*, 1810.

1. THE Commander of the Forces requests the attention of the General Officers of the army to the orders which have been often issued, relative to the detention and use of dragoons as orderlies.

2. If

2. If circumstances require that any General Officer should use dragoons to keep up a communication, he will apply for a party for that purpose, which must be sent back as soon as the purpose for which it was applied for is accomplished, and the dragoons must not be used as orderlies contrary to orders, on any account.

3. The Commander of the Forces is convinced the General Officers will see the necessity of attending to this order, in order to keep the Cavalry in a state of efficiency.

4. All General and Staff Officers, who have dragoons with them, are requested to send a return of their names, their troops, and the regiments to which they belong, to the Assistant Adjutant General of the Cavalry at Mafra.

5. Lieutenant Olferman, 97th Regiment, is to act as Brigade Major to the Duke of Brunswick's Corps, in the Honourable Colonel Pakenham's brigade, until His Majesty's pleasure is known.

6. Captain Aitcheson, 3d Guards, has the Commander of the Forces leave to proceed to England, on his promotion.

7. The following officers not having attended the Medical Board assembled at Lisbon, will be ordered to their regiments if they do not attend the next that sits.

Major Lecky, 45th Regiment.
Captain Stisted, 13th Light Dragoons.
Lieutenant Edwards, Do. Do.
——— Cotton, 88th Regiment.
——— de Bernegg, 5th Battalion 60th Regiment.
Assistant Surgeon Perston, Do. Do.
Lieutenant Ingram, 3d Battalion Royals.
Quarter Master M'Intosh, 31st Regiment.

ADJUTANT GENERAL'S OFFICE.

G. O. *Pero Negro, 18th October,* 1810.

LIEUTENANT Ingram, 1st Foot, having been reported sufficiently recovered, will join his regiment without delay.

The General Abstract for 165 days Forage Money for the army cannot be made up in consequence of many of the regimental returns not having been sent in.

The returns of the under-mentioned corps have not been received by the Quarter Master General.

3d Dragoon Guards
13th Light Dragoons.
3d Guards.
3d Regiment or Buffs.
7th do. 1st Battalion.
24th do. do.
28th do. do.
29th do. do.
30th do. do.
31st do. do.
34th do. do.
38th do. do.
39th do. do.
44th do. do.
48th do. 1st Battalion.
48th do. 2d do.
53d do. do.
57th do. do.
58th do. do.
66th do. do.
79th do. do.

87th

87th Regiment, 2d Battalion.
92d do. do.
94th do. do.
Duke of Brunswick's Infantry.
5th Line Battalion, King's German Legion.
Royal Waggon Train.
Captain Plate's Independant Company King's German Legion.

ADJUTANT GENERAL'S OFFICE,
G. O. Pero Negro, 19th October, 1810.

1. LIEUTENANT COLONEL Collins of the 83d Regiment will place himself under the orders of Marshal Beresford.

2. Officers commanding regiments are requested to send to the Military Secretary their recommendations for the vacancies that have lately occurred.

3. The Commander of the Forces requests that the Officers of the army will not shoot in the park of Mafra, without having leave to do so from the government.

ADJUTANT GENERAL'S OFFICE.
G. O. Pero Negro, 22d October, 1810.

1. CAPTAIN Mallett of the 30th Regiment is attached till further orders to the department of the Quarter Master General, and will receive his instructions from that officer.

2. Ensign de Francosa, 5th Battalion 60th Regiment, is appointed to act as Interpreter to Major General A.

 Campbell,

Campbell, from the present date; he will receive pay and allowances as Ensign, and be allowed to draw forage for a horse, agreeable to No. 12. of the General Orders of the 6th May, 1809.

3. Lieutenant Andrew Schleitter, of the 1st Line Battalion King's German Legion, is appointed to act as an Extra Aide de Camp to Major General Low, till further orders.

ADJUTANT GENERAL'S OFFICE.

G. O. *Pero Negro, 23d October, 1810.*

1. THE Commander of the Forces has observed with the greatest concern, the large number of men returned by the several regiments as sick in General Hospital, compared with the returns received from the Medical Officers, of the number of men actually on their books in the Hospitals.

2. The former, at present, is more than double the latter, and it must be owing to some existing abuse.

3. The Commander of the Forces has besides been informed by many officers commanding regiments and brigades in the army, that there are many Non-commissioned Officers and soldiers walking about the streets in Belem and Lisbon, quite recovered, while others are doing the duty of these men before the enemy in the field.

4. In order to put a stop to these abuses, the Commander of the Forces desires that the following regulations may be attended to.

5. He repeats the orders which have been so frequently issued, that no officer in the Medical department shall have any soldier from the ranks as his servant or bat

man,

man, or to attend upon him in any manner, and declares his determination to bring before a general Court Martial any officer of the Medical department who shall make use of a Non-commissioned Officer, or soldier, in any menial capacity whatever, or as a Clerk, Store Keeper, Ward Master, or Orderly, except under the following Regulations.

6. A Board to assemble at Lisbon to-morrow, to consist of, Colonel Peacocke, the Inspector General of Hospitals, and Captain M'Kenzie, the Assistant Quarter Master General, to consider of and decide upon the number of Clerks, Store-Keepers, Ward-Masters, and Orderlies from the ranks, required to attend upon the sick.

7. In considering these points, the Board will advert to the facility of obtaining the service of Portuguese Clerks, Store-Keepers, &c. at Lisbon, and they will send the return for the inspection and approbation of the Commander of the Forces.

They will also advert to the necessity that the Officers of the Medical department should themselves attend the wards of the Hospitals, and not have Non-commissioned Officers as Ward-Masters, at a period when the whole army are left at their post day and night. The Commander of the Forces must insist upon the Officers of the Medical department being at all times in the wards of the Hospitals.

8. When the necessary number of attendants in the Hospital shall be fixed, Colonel Peacocke will fix upon the names of the Non-commissioned Officers and soldiers of the several regiments, who are to be attendants in the Hospital, and he will send lists of their names to the several regiments.

9. Colonel Peacocke is requested occasionally to en-

quire respecting the number of sick and wounded in the Hospital at Lisbon, and to augment or diminish the number of attendants according to the number of sick, and according to the degree of assistance which can be procured by the employment of Portuguese attendants, reporting such increase or diminution to the Commander of the Forces, and sending lists of names of Non-commissioned Officers to be so employed or dismissed from employment, to the several regiments.

10. All men thus dismissed from employment in the Hospitals, either now or at any future period, are to be sent by the first opportunity to their regiments, and the Commander of the Forces positively forbids, that any Non-commissioned Officer or soldier shall be employed as an attendant, at the Hospitals at Lisbon or Belem, without the order of Colonel Peacocke, in his Orderly-book.

11. Non-commissioned Officers and soldiers, employed as attendants in the Hospitals, are not on any account, at any time, to quit the square of the building in which the Hospital is.

12. The soldiers when discharged from the Hospital are to be sent to the Convalescent Barracks at Belem, and it is to be understood by their Officers and them, that they are not sent there for their amusement, but that they may recover their health entirely, and return to their duty with the army. There appears therefore no occasion for their being in the streets and public houses at all hours of the day and night, but they ought to be made to lead a sober and regular life.

13. The Commander of the Forces therefore desires, that no Non-commissioned Officer or soldier in the Convalescent Barracks at Belem, may be suffered to go out of the

the barrack yard, at any time, excepting on duty in charge of an Officer or Non-commissioned Officer.

14. The Commander of the Forces refers the Commandant of the depot at Belem to the General Orders of the 17th June, 1809.

15. He likewise desires, that Non-commissioned Officers and soldiers, convalescent in the depot at Belem, may not have a ration of wine, unless the surgeon who attended them while in Hospital should recommend that they should have it for their more early recovery.

Memorandum.—Lieutenant Graham of the 71st Regiment will place himself under the orders of Marshal Beresford.

The returns for 165 days Forage Money are still wanting by the Quarter Master General, from the following Regiments.

3d Dragoon Guards.
24th Regiment.
38th do.
53d do.
66th do.
48th do. 2d Battalion.
95th do. Detachments 2d and 3d Battalion.

Regiments are reminded to send in their Monthly Returns as soon as possible after the 25th instant, and the Assistant Adjutant Generals will not fail to forward them, agreeable to the General Orders of 24th September, 1810.

G. O.

ADJUTANT GENERAL'S OFFICE.
G. O. *Pero Negro, 25th October,* 1810.

CAPTAIN Spottiswood of the 71th Regiment is appointed Aide de Camp to Major General The Honourable Charles Colville, from the date of the Major General's appointment.

Ensign Churchill, 1st Guards, is appointed an Extra Aide de Camp to Lieutenant General Hill, till further orders.

Lieutenant Price of the 43d Regiment, is appointed an Extra Aide de Camp to Major General Hoghton, till further Orders.

ADJUTANT GENERAL'S OFFICE.
G. O. *Pero Negro, 26th October,* 1810.

1. THE Commander of the Forces has directed the Commissary General to supply the troops with a certain quantity of rice till further orders.

The quantity supplied will be 1lb. among eight men, which is to be boiled up with their meat.

2. Commanding Officers of regiments will make requisitions upon the Assistant Commissaries attached to brigades for this rice, as soon as the latter shall be enabled to supply it.

3. In order to keep up the supply of cattle, the Commander of the Forces has likewise given orders that the troops shall be supplied for the present with salt meat on two days in each week.

4. The Commanding Officers of regiments will settle with the Commissaries the days on which they are to receive

ceive fresh, and those on which they are to receive salt meat.

ADJUTANT GENERAL'S OFFICE.

G. O. Pero Negro, 27th October, 1810.

1. THE following Medical Officers, having arrived from England, are placed on the strength of the staff of the army from the 24th October.

William Hogg, Deputy Inspector.

Adam Neale, Physician to the Forces.

James Forbes, Surgeon, do.

Alexander Copeland, Deputy Purveyor.

James Pattison . . .
Rodger Hanley . . .
George King . . .
Dennis Kearney . . .
John Ashwood . . .
James Chandler . . .
} Hospital Mates.

ADJUTANT GENERAL'S OFFICE.

G. O. Pero Negro, 28th October, 1810.

1. LIEUTENANT M'Donald, 71st Regiment, will place himself under the orders of Marshal Beresford.

ADJUTANT GENERAL'S OFFICE.

G. O. Pero Negro, 30th October, 1810.

1. THE Commander of the Forces has given directions, that

that an issue of a blanket for two men of the Non-commissioned Officers and rank and file may be made to the several regiments, and the Commanding Officers of regiments will as soon as possible send to the Quarter Master General returns of the number of blankets which they will require for this proportion for the effective men.

The regiments which retained their blankets in the month of June last, will of course receive none, but the Commander of the Forces requests that the Commanding Officers of those regiments will send to the Quarter Master General a return of the number of great coats they have in store, and will make application for means of transport to have them brought up to their regiments, and issue them to the men to whom they belong.

The regiment will likewise make a return of the number of great coats wanting to complete every Non-commissioned Officer and soldier with a great coat.

ADJUTANT GENERAL'S OFFICE.

G. A. O. *Pero Negro, 30th October*, 1810.

SERJEANT Crane, 74th Regiment, is dismissed from his situation as Assistant Provost Marshal to the army, and will return to his regiment, being reported by the Commandant at Lisbon to be often in a state of intoxication and incapable of doing his duty.

ADJUTANT GENERAL'S OFFICE.

G. O. *Pero Negro, 1st November*, 1810.

Memorandum.—CAPTAIN Cooksey of the 79th Regiment,

ment, and Lieutenant Weatley of the 50th Regiment, are to place themselves under the orders of Marshal Beresford.

The returns called for in the orders of the 30th October are to be sent in with the least possible delay.

G. A. O.

The Spanish troops are to fire three vollies of musquetry in their cantonments at Enaxara de los Caballeros to-morrow, a little after one p. m. on the occasion of taking the oath of fidelity to the Cortes of Spain.

Adjutant General's Office.
G. O. *Pero Negro, 1st November,* 1810.

A General Court Martial will assemble at Caxara tomorrow morning te 9 o'clock, for the trial of such prisoners as may be brought before it.

Colonel The Honourable Edward Pakenham, President; members to be furnished equally by the 4th and 6th Divisions of Infantry.

Names and dates of Commissions and list of evidences to be sent in to the Deputy Judge Advocate at Caxara as soon as possible.

Adjutant General's Office.
G. A. O. *Pero Negro, 2d November,* 1810.

At a General Court Martial held by virtue of a warrant and in pursuance of an order from his Excellency

Lieutenant

Lieutenant General Lord Viscount Wellington, K. B. Commander of the Forces, James Mulligan, private soldier in the 27th Regiment, was tried;

For quitting his post while on sentry, between the hours of eight and nine o'clock, on the 24th October or thereabouts, being then on sentry, and deserting towards the enemy. To which charge the Prisoner pleaded not guilty. The Court proceeded to the examination of witnesses, and having maturely and deliberately weighed and considered the evidence adduced in support of the prosecution against the prisoner, together with what he has offered in his defence, are of opinion that he is guilty of the charge preferred against him, (being in breach of the Articles of War,) and do by virtue thereof sentence him the Prisoner, James Mulligan, of the 27th Regiment, to be shot to death at such time and place as his Excellency the Commander of the Forces may deem fit.

Which sentence has been confirmed by his Excellency the Commander of the Forces.

The Commander of the Forces is pleased to direct that the foregoing sentence on Private James Mulligan of the 27th Regiment may be carried into execution to-morrow morning early, in presence of the 27th Regiment and two Companies of each regiment of the Honorable Major General Cole's and Major General Campbell's divisions paraded for that purpose under the direction of the Assistant Provosts of those divisions and the superintendance of the Officer Commanding the 27th Regiment.

G. O.

ADJUTANT GENERAL'S OFFICE.
G. O. Pero Negro, 3d November, 1810.

1. THE Commander of the Forces desires the Commanding Officer of the depot at Belem may be ordered to warn Lieutenant Sedgewick of the 2d Battalion 5th Regiment of the necessity of attending more particularly to his duty when he shall march with a detachment of convalescents in future. The excuses he has made for bringing up 29 men out of 41 placed under his command are frivolous, and by his own account many of the men said to be unable to march, have since joined the army under another Officer.

2. The Commanding Officer of the depot at Belem will report if Lieutenant Sedgewick had a copy of the orders of 24th June, 1809, relative to the march of detachments.

Serjeant Joseph Steward of the 97th, and Serjeant William Gledhill, of the 53d Regiments, are appointed Assistant Provost Marshals to the army, and are to be stationed at Belem till further orders.

ADJUTANT GENERAL'S OFFICE.
A. G. O. Pero Negro, 3d November, 1810.

Memorandum.—DIVINE Service will be performed at Cadaciera, the Head Quarters of Major General Picton's division, to-morrow morning at nine o'clock.

ADJUTANT GENERAL'S OFFICE.
G. O. Pero Negro, 4th November, 1810.

1. THE Commander of the Forces is concerned to hear that

that some Officers of the army have forgotten their own situation so far as to threaten the Serjeant Postmaster at Lisbon.

2. It is to be understood that the Serjeant Postmaster at Lisbon is not obliged to send letters from the office to any body excepting the Commandant, Assistant Adjutant General, and Assistant Quarter Master General, and Officer commanding the depôt. The other officers at Lisbon must send to him for their letters after the bags are duly sorted, and not before; and Colonel Peacocke is requested to protect the Postmaster from the violence or impatience of any individual.

An officer from each of the undermentioned brigades will be sent without delay to take charge of the convalescents of the depôt at Belem, conformable to the General Orders of 13th June, 1809.

Brigades.

Major General Lumley's,
Brigadier General Crawford's,
Honourable Colonel Pakenham's,
Major General Sir William Erskine's,
The Brigade consisting of the 4th, 30th, and 44th Regiments.

ADJUTANT GENERAL'S OFFICE.

G. O. *Pero Negro, 5th November*, 1810.

1. THE Commander of the Forces desires that, when Paymasters or Quarter Masters, or other Officers of regiments are sent to Lisbon on duty, they may not take detachments

tachments of Non-commissioned Officers and soldiers with them.

2. The depôt at Belem will always furnish the men which are required for any fatigue duty which they may require to be performed.

3. Officers and others allowed servants, who proceed to Lisbon on duty, or on account of their health, if allowed to take with them their servants, should not be allowed to retain those soldiers who are able to do their duty. There are at Belem men belonging to every regiment in the army not fit to do their duty in the field, who should be employed as servants to Officers and others who, on account of duty or health, are obliged to remain at Lisbon or Belem.

4. When any Officer proceeds to Lisbon with a detachment, or with only one soldier as his servant, he must make a nominal return of the detachment, or send the soldier's name to the Officer commanding the depôt of convalescents at Belem.

5. A Board, consisting of Colonel Peacocke, Colonel Darrock, and Captain Tucker to assemble at Lisbon, on Friday, the 9th instant, to enquire into certain matters which will be referred to them by the Commander of the Forces.

The Judge Advocate General will attend this Board.

6. Major General Dunlop having arrived at Lisbon, is to command the Brigade of Infantry in the 5th Division, consisting of the 4th, 2d Battalion 30th, and 2d Battalion 44th Regiments; appointment dated 19th September, 1810.

Captain Davies, 1st Foot Guards, is appointed Aide de

Camp to Major General Dunlop, from 19th September, 1810.

Brevet Major Gordon, 3d Guards, is appointed Aide de Camp to the Commander of the Forces on the establishment from the 25th October.

Captain Bainbridge, 93d Regiment, is appointed Deputy Assistant Quarter Master General from 18th September, 1810.

ADJUTANT GENERAL'S OFFICE.

G. O. *Pero Negro, 7th November*, 1810.

1. A BOARD, consisting of Lieutenant Colonel Langley, R. W. T. President, and two Captains of the depôt, at Belem, to assemble on Friday morning at Lisbon to investigate certain circumstances that will be referred to them by the Commander of the Forces.

2. The following letter has been received by His Excellency the Commander of the Forces, which he directs a strict attention will be paid to by the Army under his command.

(Copy.

HORSE GUARDS,
28th September, 1810.

MY LORD,

IT having been represented to the Commander in Chief that great delay arises in the settlement of the accompts of men who arrive in this country from foreign stations, from their not being accompanied with the proper returns of the periods for which they have been paid abroad:

Sir

Sir David Dundas desires that your Lordship will be pleased to give your consideration to this subject, and that special care may be taken for the time to come that no men are permitted to embark from your Lordship's command for England without the return prescribed by the regulations of the 24th October, 1808.

(Signed) H. TORRENS,
Military Secretary.

Lieut. General
Lord Viscount Wellington,
&c. &c. &c.

3. Lieutenant Dundas, 5th Regiment, is appointed to act as Brigadier Major to the troops under the command of Major General Sontag, from 1st September, 1810.

ADJUTANT GENERAL'S OFFICE.
G. O. *Pero Negro, 10th November,* 1810.

1. THE Commander of the Forces is concerned to have received reports from some of the regiments of the desertion of British soldiers to the enemy; a crime which, in all his experience in the British service, in different parts of the world, was till lately unknown in it; and the existence of which, at the present moment, he can attribute only to some false hopes held out to these unfortunate criminal persons.

The British soldiers cannot but be aware of the difference between their situation and that of the enemy opposed to them, and the miserable tale told by the half-starved wretches whom they see daily coming into their lines, ought alone, exclusive of their sense of honour and patriotism, to be sufficient to deter them from participating their miserable fate.

However, although the Commander of the Forces laments the fate of the unfortunate soldiers who have committed this crime, he is determined that they shall feel the cousequence of it during their lives, and that they shall never return to their friends or their homes.

He accordingly reqnests that the Commanding Officers of regiments from which any soldier has deserted to the enemy, will as soon as possible send to the Adjutant General's Office a description of his person, together with an account when he was inlisted with the regiment, where born, and to what parish he belongs, in order that the friends of these soldiers may be made acquainted with the crime which they have committed; may be prepared to consider them as lost for ever, and may deliver them up to justice in case they should ever return to their native country.

2. Captain Diggle, of the 52d Regiment, has the Commander of the Forces' leave to join the 2d Battalion of his regiment in England to which he belongs.

Memorandum.—Divine Service will be performed tomorrow morning at Cadoira, at 8 o'clock a. m. Major General Picton's Brigade to attend.

Colonel M'Kinnon's will parade for the same purpose at 10 o'clock, a. m. at the Head Quarters of the brigade.

ADJUTANT GENERAL'S OFFICE.

G. O. *Pero Negro, 12th November,* 1810.

1. THE 1st Battalion 23d Regiment, being arrived, is to be in the brigade of Infantry, in the 4th Division, commanded

manded by the Honourable Colonel Pakenham, till further orders.

2. The Brunswick Light Infantry are to be attached to the Light Division, until further orders.

3. This corps is to detach one company to do duty with the Light Infantry of Colonel Pakenham's Brigade, and two companies to do duty with the Light Infantry of Major General Dunlop's and Brigadier General Hay's Brigade, in the 5th Division.

4. The Commander of the Forces refers the General Officers commanding divisions and brigades, to his orders on the formation and use of Light Infantry Battalions in each brigade, and he desires that they may be strictly adhered to: he again recommends the detached companies of the 5th Battalion 60th Regiment, and those now detached from the Brunswick Light Infantry, to their care and attention, and desires that these companies, when not in battalions with the Light Infantry Companies of the regiment, in the manner and at the time pointed out in the General Orders, may be kept at the Head Quarters of the brigade.

5. Brigade Major Olferman, attached to Colonel Pakenham, is to be attached to the Light Division until further orders.

6. Lieutenant Baron Osten, 16th Light Dragoons, is appointed to act as Brigade Major to Colonel De Grey's Brigade of Heavy Cavalry till His Majesty's pleasure is known.

7. Captain White, 13th Light Dragoons, is appointed a Deputy Assistant Quarter Master General until His Majesty's pleasure is known.

ADJUTANT GENERAL'S OFFICE.

G. O. *Pero Negro*, 14*th November*, 1810.

1. LIEUTENANT COLONEL Reynele, 71st Regiment, is appointed an Assistant in the Adjutant General's Department until His Majesty's pleasure is known. He will be attached until further orders to the 4th Division of Infantry.

2. Captain Craig, Deputy Assistant Adjutant General, is removed from the 4th Division to do duty with the corps of Seamen and Marines, &c. at Alhandra.

3. Colonel Hulse, of the Coldstream Guards, is appointed to act as Colonel on the Staff until His Majesty's pleasure is known, and is to command the Brigade of Infantry, in the 6th Division, under the directions of Major General A. Campbell, until further orders.

4. Colonel Wynch, of the 4th, or King's own Regiment of Infantry, is appointed to act as Colonel on the Staff until His Majesty's pleasure is known, and is to command the Brigade of Infantry hitherto under the command of Lieutenant Colonel Barclay, until further orders.

5. Colonel Peacock will send Ensign Larbush, of the 5th Battalion 60th Regiment, without delay to his corps, as the Medical Board have reported that he has no complaint whatever which will prevent his doing his duty.

Memorandum.

Lieutenant Turner, 11th Regiment,
Lieutenant Lenon 27th do.

are to place themselves under the orders of Marshal Sir William Carr Beresford.

6. The Court Martial, of which the Honourable Colonel Pakenham was President, is dissolved.

G. O.

ADJUTANT GENERAL'S OFFICE.

G. O. *Alenquer*, 16*th November*, 1810.

1. THE Commander of the Forces requests that when any of the General Officers quit their quarters, if only to take a ride, they will leave at home some person to receive, open, and carry into execution any orders that may be sent to them.

2. The Commander of the Forces requests the Officers commanding Regiments will be very cautious in occupying the quarters in which the French troops may have been quartered, to make their men clean them well out before they sleep in them; and, if possible, to have fires lighted in them, but care must be taken not to burn the houses.

These precautions will be found to contribute much, to preserve the health of the Soldiers.

3. The allowance of rice, which has been given to the troops lately, must of necessity be discontinued as soon as the Assistant Commissaries will have issued that which they have with their several brigades.

ADJUTANT GENERAL'S OFFICE,

G. O. *Alenquer*, 17*th November*, 1810.

1. THE Commander of the Forces directs that the corps of Guides shall be augmented, and the establishment of mounted men to be in future—

Lieutenants	Cornets	Serjeants	Corporals	Trumpeters	Privates
6	6	8	8	2	50

and Captain Scovell, Deputy Assistant Quarter Master General, will take measures to complete them as soon as possible.

 2. The

2. The Brunswick Light Infantry is to be in Colonel Wynch's Brigade, in the Light Division.

3. The 61st Regiment is to be in Colonel Hulse's Brigade, in the 6th Division.

4. The 2d Battalion Fusileers is to be in the Honourable Colonel Pakenham's Brigade, in the 4th Division.

5. The Cavalry and horses of the army must not be put into any stables or places which have been occupied by the enemy, without very carefully cleaning and washing the mangers, &c. to take every precaution against glanders.

ADJUTANT GENERAL'S OFFICE.

G. O. *Cartaxo, 23d November*, 1810.

1. THE Commander of the Forces requests that the Commanding Officers of Regiments will inform the Soldiers that the wine casks are a most valuable property to the people of this country, and he desires that they may not be destroyed.

2. The Paymasters of Regiments are to send to Loures to receive the balances due on their estimates to the 24th instant.

ADJUTANT GENERAL'S OFFICE.

G. O. *Cartaxo, 24th November*, 1810.

(Copy.) HORSE GUARDS.

October 25, 1810.

MY LORD,

1. HAVING had the honour to lay before the King the proceedings of a General Court Martial, held at Lisbon, on the 28th of August, 1810, and subsequent

quent days, for the trial of Hospital Mate Henry Miles Goulding, who was arraigned upon the undermentioned charges, viz.

1st. For scandalous and infamous conduct unbecoming the character of an officer and a gentleman, in embezzling various stores, the property of Government, intended for patients in General Hospitals, and converting them to his own private use.

2d. For disobedience of orders in employing Private Thomas Fielding, of the 97th Regiment, as his private servant when attached as an orderly to the General Hospital.

Upon which charges the Court came to the following decision:

The Court having maturely considered the evidence against the prisoner, together with what has been produced in his defence, is of opinion that he, the said Hospital Mate, Henry Miles Goulding, is guilty of the whole of the first charge and partly of the second charge, namely: although not employing an orderly, yet guilty of keeping a soldier, who at the time a patient in hospital, as his servant. The Court, therefore, finding that a misapplication and embezzlement of Hospital Stores, the property of Government, has been uninterruptedly carried on by Hospital Mate Henry Miles Goulding, and converted to his private use, from the 25th April to the 14th July, with the exceptions of only a few articles, for seven days, as also guilty of disobedience of orders in keeping a soldier, (a patient in hospital, as his servant; which being in breach of the Articles of War, do therefore sentence him, the said Henry Miles Goulding, to be dismissed His Majesty's service; and further to forfeit the sum of One Hundred

Pounds

Pounds sterling, to be levied and disposed of as directed by the ninety-first clause of the Mutiny Act.

I am to acquaint your Lordship that His Majesty was pleased to approve and confirm so much of the finding and sentence of the Court as adjudges the prisoner to be dismissed His Majesty's service.

Your Lordship will therefore acquaint me with the day upon which the sentence is made known to Mr. Goulding, as from that day he will cease to receive pay in His Majesty's service.

I have the honour to be,

(Signed) DAVID DUNDAS,

Commander in Chief.

Lieutenant General

Lord Wellington, K. B.

&c. &c. &c.

2. Captain Appleton, of the 57th Regiment, has the Commander of the Forces' leave to join the 2d Battalion of his regiment in Jersey.

ADJUTANT GENERAL'S OFFICE,

G. O. *Cartaxo, 25th November,* 1810.

Memorandum.—Heads of departments will send in to the Adjutant General's Office on this day, or as soon after as possible, nominal returns of the officers at present serving in their respective departments, specifying the regiments to which they belong, and the names of the places at which they are stationed.

The Assistant Adjutant General, attached to divisions, will send in to the Adjutant General's Office this day or as

soon

soon after as possible, nominal returns of the General and other Staff Officers at present serving in their respective divisions, specifying the nature of their appointments, regiments and stations, and to note at the bottom any alterations which have taken place during the preceding month.

Colonel Darrock, Assistant Adjutant General, will likewise send in a return of the General and Staff Officers at Lisbon.

Regiments and Corps will also send in their monthly returns for the 25th instant, as soon as possible.

ADJUTANT GENERAL'S OFFICE.

G. O. *Cartaxo, 26th November,* 1810.

1. MAJOR GENERAL Cameron has the Commander of the Forces' leave of absence to proceed to Lisbon, and from thence to England for the recovery of his health.

2. The Commander of the Forces requests that the General Officers and Commanding Officers of Regiments will take measures to prevent the soldiers from using the doors and windows, and pulling down the timbers of the houses for fire wood.

The consequence will be that the soldiers will be without quarters, besides the serious injury that these practices occasion to the inhabitants of the country.

3. Applications of Officers to serve in the Portuguese Army will be forwarded through the Officers commanding Corps and Generals of Brigades and Divisions to the Adjutant General.

G. O.

ADJUTANT GENERAL'S OFFICE.

G. O. *Cartaxo, 27th November,* 1810.

1. THE Commander of the Forces reminds the Commanding Officers of regiments of the inconvenience which the troops have experienced from the want of salt, occasionally during the campaign, and he urges them and the Officers commanding companies, to make their men take care of the salt which they receive occasionally with their salt meat.

Salt is to be procured at the salt pans at Alberca, upon the Tagus.

ADJUTANT GENERAL'S OFFICE.

G. O. *Cartaxo, 28th November,* 1810.

1. ALL letters and applications, hitherto addressed to the Military Secretary, must in future be addressed to Lord Fitzroy Somerset, by whom all warrants will be countersigned till further orders.

ADJUTANT GENERAL'S OFFICE.

G. O. *Cartaxo, 29th November,* 1810.

1. MAJOR Laurie, A. D. C. to Major General Cameron, may proceed to England with the Major General on his promotion.

3. Captain Wood, Coldstream Guards, may proceed to England, having given in his resignation.

G. O.

ADJUTANT GENERAL'S OFFICE.

G. O. *Cartaxo, 4th December, 1810.*

1. THE Commissary General will give directions that the troops may receive rice in the same proportions as ordered by the General Orders of the 26th October, 1810, as soon as the Assistant Commissaries of brigades can issue it to them.

ADJUTANT GENERAL'S OFFICE.

G. O. *Cartaxo, 5th December, 1810.*

1. THE Commander of the Forces requests that the General Officers and the Commanding Officers of Regiments will take measures to prevent the troops under their command from cutting the olive and other fruit trees for fire wood.

2. Parties on fatigue from each regiment should be sent out every morning to cut the quantity of wood required for fires; and as there is no want of fire wood in the neighbourhood of all the cantonments, there can be no occasion for cutting the olive trees for that purpose.

ADJUTANT GENERAL'S OFFICE.

G. O. *Cartaxo, 7th December, 1810.*

LIEUTENANT Watson, Royal Dragoons, is to place himself under the orders of Marshal Sir William Carr Beresford.

Lieutenant M'Namara and Ensign Mitchell, of the 9th Regiment, are to place themselves under the orders of Marshal Sir William Carr Beresford.

G. O.

ADJUTANT GENERAL'S OFFICE.
G. O. *Cartaxo, 8th December,* 1810.

1. THE Commander of the Forces having perused the proceedings of a Court of Enquiry, of which Colonel Langley was President, has written to the Commissary General, a Letter on the subject of that enquiry, of which the following is an extract.

Cartaxo, 3d December, 1810.

I ENCLOSE the proceedings of a Court of Enquiry which has been held on a statement made by Mr. Deputy Commissary Dunmore, on the conduct of Mr. Berkeley.

This gentleman was represented to me, in the course of the summer, as having made a great exertion to supply the Officers and soldiers of the Army, with various articles of necessaries which they required, and as being likely, according to the appearance of the state of affairs at that moment, to incur very large losses.

I was induced, therefore, and on account of the very favourable opinion entertained of Mr. Berkeley, by Colonel Pakenham, Sir William Myers, and others, to give directions that assistance might be given to Mr. Berkeley, to enable him to transport his stores to the army, "at his own expence;" and that if the Commissariat should want any of the articles of supply which he had brought out, they might be purchased from him, rather than from other persons, provided he sold them of an equally good quality, and at an equally cheap rate.

I observe from the proceedings of the Court of Enquiry, that a construction has been given to these directions, which they were never intended to bear, they were intended

to

to be applied solely to those articles which Mr. Berkeley had then at Lisbon, of which it was my wish, that he should have an opportunity of disposing, as it had been represented to me, that he had been encouraged by different Officers of the Army to bring them out. It has been understood, however, as it appears both by Mr. Deputy Commissary Dunmore, and Mr. Berkeley, that these orders were intended to apply not only to what Mr. Berkeley had at the time landed at Lisbon, but to whatever goods of any description, which he might hereafter import into Portugal, thus giving Mr. Berkeley a description of monopoly of the consumption of the British Army; and this gentleman has in fact taken advantage of this erroneous construction given to these orders, by importing wines and other articles, to which they were never intended to apply, and offering them for sale to the Commissariat.

I now desire that it may be understood, that these orders are entirely countermanded, and I will have nothing to do with Mr. Berkeley.

I beg also that you will inform Mr. Deputy Commissary Dunmore, that I approve entirely of his having made the statement respecting the conduct of Mr. Berkeley, which has been the subject of enquiry.

Memorandum.—Major Dishon, 43d Regiment, may proceed to England, to join the 2d Battalion of that corps.

ADJUTANT GENERAL'S OFFICE.

G. O. *Cartaxo, 9th December,* 1810.

1. THE Commander of the Forces has received the orders

ders of the Commander in Chief, to appoint Lieutenant Colonel Clifton, of the 3d Dragoon Guards, to do duty as Lieutenant Colonel of the Royal Dragoons, until His Majesty's pleasure is known.

A. G. O.

Lieutenant Lovat, of the 50th Regiment, is to place himself under the orders of Marshal Sir William Carr Beresford.

ADJUTANT GENERAL'S OFFICE.

G. O.

Cartaxo, 12th December, 1810.

1. A GENERAL Court Martial will assemble at Chamusca, on the 15th instant, Major General Houghton, President; the members to be furnished by the 2d Division of Infantry, with the exception of the Officers of the 2d Battalion 48th Regiment.

2. The Commander of the Forces is concerned to learn, that notwithstanding his repeated orders, and the inconvenience which all the Officers and soldiers have experienced, from the practice of burning doors and windows, and the furniture and materials of houses, it still continues, and within these few days, the furniture and doors in the Quinta of the Duke of La Foens in the neighbourhood of Alcontrenha, and Alcoentre, has been carried off and burnt.

3. The Commander of the Forces is ashamed to acknowledge, that the British troops have, in many instances, done more mischief to the country in this manner, than had been done by the enemy.

4. The necessity of repeating orders is the strongest proof

proof of the want of discipline in the troops, and of attention in the Officers, who have it in their power if they do their duty, to prevent these practices; and the Commander of the Forces declares it to be his intention, to report to His Majesty, the name of the Commanding Officer and Officers of any regiment by the soldiers of which these practices may be committed in future.

Memorandum.—Ensign Farden, 5th Regiment, may proceed to England, having given in his resignation.

Lieutenant Schlutter, King's German Legion, may proceed to England, being reported unfit for any Military duty.

Captain Campbell, and Captain Davidson, 42d Regiment, may proceed to England to join the 1st Battalion.

Lieutenant Gibbons, 7th Regiment, being reported fit for duty, is to join his regiment forthwith.

Captain J. Thomas Jones, Royal Engineers, is appointed to act on the Staff of the Army, as Major of Brigade to that department.

ADJUTANT GENERAL'S OFFICE.

G. O. *Cartaxo, 13th December,* 1810.

THE following Officers are to place themselves under the orders of Marshal Sir William Carr Beresford.

Lieutenant Fisher, 40th Regiment.
Lieutenant Stewart, 40th do.
Lieutenant Brackenbury, 61st Regiment.

Major Reh, being promoted in the 4th Battalion King's German Legion, now in Sicily, has the Commander of the Forces leave to proceed thither.

 Promo-

Promotions in the Corps of Guides.

Antonio Belfont de Burgos }
Agostino Albano de Silviera }

serving in the Corps of Mounted Guides, as Cornets, are appointed to serve as Lieutenants in the said Corps, from the 25th November, with pay and allowances of Lieutenants of Cavalry.

Antonio Joachim de Oliviera }
Antonio Arnado . . . }

are appointed to serve as Cornets in the said Corps from the 25th November, with pay and allowances of Cornets of Cavalry.

ADJUTANT GENERAL'S OFFICE.
G. O. *Cartaxo, 14th December,* 1810.

CAPTAIN Nelson is appointed to act as Assistant Commissary with the 3d Division, in the room of Mr. Francis M'Donald, who has been permitted to resign his situation in the Commissariat department.

Captain Dalton, 4th Dragoons, has the Commander of the Forces leave to proceed to England, to join the Depot Squadron.

ADJUTANT GENERAL'S OFFICE.
G. O. *Cartaxo, 15th December,* 1810.

MAJOR Offley, of the 23d Fusileers, will place himself under the orders of Marshal Sir William Carr Beresford.

G. O.

ADJUTANT GENERAL'S OFFICE.

G. O. *Cartaxo*, 18*th December*, 1810.

THE Rev. Mr. Scott, Chaplain to the Forces, has the Commander of the Forces leave to return to England for two months, on very urgent private affairs.

A General Court Martial will assemble on Friday, the 21st instant, at Azambuja, for the trial of such prisoners as may be brought before it.

Major General The Honourable C. Colville, President.

The Members to be furnished by the 4th Division of Infantry.

ADJUTANT GENERAL'S OFFICE.

G. O. *Cartaxo*, 20*th December*, 1810.

Assistant Surgeon Hooper, 19th Regiment,
———— M'Donell, 19th Regiment,
———— Jones, 2d Ceylon Regiment,
are to proceed to England, for the purpose of joining their regiments.

ADJUTANT GENERAL'S OFFICE.

G. O. *Cartaxo*, 21*st December*, 1810.

LIEUTENANT Blake, of the 2d Battalion 66th Regiment, is to place himself under the orders of Marshal Sir William Carr Beresford.

Captain Cuthbert, 7th Royal Fusileers, is appointed Aide de Camp to Major General Picton, from 24th ultimo, vice Captain Sir Orford Gordon, who resigns that situation.

ADJUTANT GENERAL'S OFFICE.

G. O. *Cartaxo, 22d December*, 1810.

CAPTAIN Chapman, Royal Engineers, has the Commander of the Forces leave to proceed to England, on his appointment as Private Secretary to the Master General of the Ordnance.

ADJUTANT GENERAL'S OFFICE.

G. O. *Cartaxo, 23d December*, 1810.

1. THE Commander of the Forces has frequently been obliged to request the Officers of the army would not shoot the deer in the Royal or other parks, without having leave to do so; but he is concerned to learn, that the practice still continues in a great degree, in the Duchess de la Foen's park, near the cantonments of the army.

2. The Commander of the Forces will avoid to name the regiments, by the Officers of which this has been done; but he requests those officers to reflect, that their continuing to shoot the deer in these parks, is not only a breach of military discipline, but shews an entire forgetfulness of the rights of property, which they would be obliged to respect in their own country, and which they ought to respect in these, where every individual of the British Army has been so well treated.

3. The Commander of the Forces is not desirous of preventing the Officers of the army from amusing themselves, in any manner they may think proper, or which may be consistent with their duty, but he requests them to respect the parks and preserves of the Prince, and other inhabitants.

G. O.

ADJUTANT GENERAL'S OFFICE
G. O. *Cartaxo, 24th December,* 1810.

1. A GENERAL Court Martial will assemble at Lisbon, on the 28th instant.

Colonel Minet, 30th Regiment, President.

The Members to be furnished by the garrison at Lisbon, and from the Depot at Belem.

2. The Paymasters of regiments are to proceed to Alverca, to receive the balances due on their Estimates, to the 24th instant inclusive.

The following Officers have the Commander of the Forces leave to join the Depot of the King's German Legion in England, and will repair to Lisbon, applying to the Assistant Quarter Master General for a passage.

Captain Lodders, 5th Battalion King's German Legion.
——— Dohren, 7th . . do. . . do.
Lieutenant Hodenberg, 1st do. . . do.
——— Wessel, 2d . . do. . . do.
——— Bergėr, 5th . do. . . do.

Doctor James M'Dougle, Physician to the Forces, having arrived from England, is placed on the Staff of the army from this date.

ADJUTANT GENERAL'S OFFICE.
G. O. *Cartaxo, 26th December,* 1810.

1. AT a General Court Martial held by virtue of a warrant and in pursuance of an order from His Excellency Lord Viscount Wellington, K. B. Commander of the Forces, at Chamusca, 23d December, 1810; whereof Major General D. Houghton, was President;

John Fowler, Richard Leach, and Thomas Turner, Privates in the 2d Battalion 34th Regiment, were arraigned;

For being out of Quarters after hours, on the evening of the 8th of December, 1810, and committing a robbery on the highway in the neighbourhood of Almarim, and taking from the person of a native a bag of dollars, on the above-mentioned evening.

To which charge the prisoners pleaded not guilty, and the Court having maturely considered the evidence against the prisoners, and what they have stated in their defence, are of opinion they are not guilty of the 1st part of the charge, namely,

For being out of Quarters after hours on the evening of the 8th of December, 1810.

And further, that there is not sufficient evidence to substantiate the 2d part of the charge, against the prisoners John Fowler, and Richard Leach, namely,

Committing a robbery on the highway, in the neighbourhood of Almarim, and taking from the person of a native a bag of dollars, on the above-mentioned evening, and do therefore acquit them of the same.

The Court is further of opinion, that the prisoner Thomas Turner is guilty of the 2d part of the said charge, and do therefore sentence him, Thomas Turner, to be transported as a felon for life.

Which sentence has been confirmed by his Excellency the Commander of the Forces.

2. The Commander of the Forces pardons Thomas Turner, but he recommends to these soldiers to beware of such practices in future, they may be certain they cannot commit outrages of the description of that for which they have been tried, without being discovered, and that a perseverance

severance in the idle and dissolute habits which are the cause of them, must bring them to an ignominious end.

3. At a General Court Martial, held by virtue of a warrant and in pursuance of an order from his Excellency Lieutenant General Lord Viscount Wellington, K. B. Commander of the Forces, at Azambuja, 22d December, 1810, whereof Major General the Honourable Charles Colville was President;

Patrick Murray, of the 88th Regiment, was arraigned for desertion on or about the 25th of August, 1809.

To which charge the prisoner pleaded not guilty, and the Court having maturaly considered the evidence against the prisoner, together with what he has offered in his defence, are of opiniou that he is guilty of the crime laid to his charge, being in breach of the Articles of War, and do therefore sentence him to receive One Thousand Lashes, at such time and place as his Excellency the Commander of the Forces may think fit.

Which sentence has been confirmed by his Excellency the Commander of the Forces.

4. The sentence of the General Court Martial on Patrick Murray, of the 88th Regiment, is to be carried into execution on the 29th instant, by the Provost attached to the 3d Division, and in presence of the 88th and 5th Regiments, to be paraded for that purpose.

5. At a General Court Martial, held by virtue of a warrant and in pursuance of an order from Lieutenant General Lord Viscount Wellington, K. B. Commander of the Forces, at Azambuja, 23d December, 1810, of which Major General the Honourable C. Colville was President;

Privates Sterence Masterson and John Harris of the 5th Regiment, were arraigned;

For desertion on or about the 1st of July, 1810.

To which charge the prisoners pleaded not guilty: and the Court having maturely and deliberately considered the evidence against the prisoners, Privates Sterence Masterson and John Harris, together with what they have offered in their defence, are of opinion they are guilty of the crime laid to their charge, being in breach of the Articles of War, and do therefore sentence them to receive One Thousand Lashes each, at such time and place as his Excellency the Commander of the Forces may think fit.

Which sentence has been confirmed by his Excellency the Commander of the Forces.

6. The sentence of the general Court Martial on Sterence Masterson and John Harris, is to be carried into execution by the Provost attached to the 3d Division, in presence of the 5th and 88th Regiments, to be paraded for that purpose on the 29th instant.

Memorandum.—Paymaster M. D. Fraser, who has been appointed Paymaster to the 2d Battalion 43d Regiment, may proceed to England, to join that battalion to which he belongs.

Adjutant General's Office.

G. O. *Cartaxo, 27th December,* 1810.

1. At a General Court Martial held by virtue of a warrant and in pursuance of an order from his Excellency Lieutenant General Lord Viscount Wellington, K. B. Commander of the Forces, at Azambuja, 26th December, 1810, whereof Major General the Honourable C. Colville was President, and Captain Goodman, Deputy Judge Advo-

Advocate, was arraigned Private John Lacey, of the 58th Regiment;

For desertion on or about the 28th of November last.

To which charge the prisoner pleaded not guilty, and the Court having considered the evidence adduced against the prisoner, Private John Lacey of the 58th Regiment, together with what he has offered in his defence, are of opinion that he is guilty of the charge preferred against him, being in breach of the Articles of War, and do by virtue thereof sentence him to receive a punishment of One Thousand Lashes, at such time and place as his Excellency the Commander of the Forces may deem fit.

Which sentence has been confirmed by his Excellency the Commander of the Forces.

2. John Lacey is to be sent to the 2d Battalion 58th Regiment, and the sentence of the General Martial is to be carried into execution by the Assistant Provost attached to the 5th Division, on Monday, the 31st instant, in presence of the 58th Regiment, to be paraded for that purpose.

3. At a general Court Martial held by virtue of a warrant and pursuance of an order from his Excellency Lord Viscount Wellington, K. B. Commander of the Forces, at Azambuja, 23d December, 1810, of which Major General the Honourable C. Colville was President, and Captain Goodman Deputy Judge Advocate, was arraigned Private Robert Roberts of the 9th Regiment;

For desertion on or about the 7th of January, 1809.

To which charge the prisoner pleaded not guilty; and the Court having considered the evidence adduced against the prisoner, Private Robert Roberts of the 9th Regiment, together with what he has offered in his defence, are of opinion

opinion he is not guilty of the charge preferred against him, and do acquit him of the same.

Which decision has been confirmed by his Excellency the Commander of the Forces.

4. Private Robert Roberts is to be released from confinement, and to be sent to join the 9th Regiment.

5. At a General Court Martial held by virtue of a warrant and in pursuance of an order from his Excellency Lieutenant General Lord Viscount Wellington, K. B. Commander of the Forces, at Azambuja, 24th December, 1810, of which Major General the Honourable C. Colville was President, and Captain Goodman, Deputy Judge Advocate, was arraigned Private John Muckoloff, of the 7th Line Battalion King's German Legion;

For desertion on or about the 10th of September, 1810.

To which charge the prisoner pleaded not guilty, and the Court having considered the evidence adduced against the prisoner Private John Muckoloff, of the 7th Line Battalion King's German Legion, together with his defence, are of opinion that he is guilty of having absented himself from his regiment on the day specified in the charge, being in breach of the Articles of War, and do by virtue thereof sentence him to receive Three Hundred Lashes in the usual manner.

Which sentence has been confirmed by his Excellency the Commander of the Forces.

6. Private John Muckoloff is to be sent to the 7th Line Battalion King's German Legion, to which battalion orders will be sent respecting him.

7. The General Court Martial of which Major General D. Houghton is Prisident is adjourned, and the members may return to their duty with their several regiments and brigades.

G. O.

ADJUTANT GENERAL'S OFFICE.

G. O. *Cartaxo, 29th December*, 1810.

1. AT a General Court Martial held by virtue of a warrant and in pursuance of an order from his Excellency Lieutenant General Lord Viscount Wellington, K. B. Commander of the Forces, at Azambuja, 28th December, 1810, of which Major General the Honourable C. Colville was President, and Captain Goodman Deputy Judge Advocate, Private Conrad Bettles, of the 7th Line Battalion King's German Legion, was arraigned;

For desertion on or about the 11th August, 1810.

To which charge the Prisoner pleaded not guilty, and the Court having considered the evidence adduced in the prosecution against the prisoner, Private Conrad Bettles of the 7th Line Battalion King's German Legion, together with what he has submitted in his defence, are of opinion that he is guilty of the charge preferred against him, being in breach of the Articles of War and do by virtue thereof sentence him to receive a punishment of One Thousand Lashes, at such time as his Excellency the Commander of the Forces may deem fit.

Which sentence has been confirmed by his Excellency the Commander of the Forces.

2. Private Conrad Bettles is to be sent to his regiment, and the sentence of the General Court Martial is to be carried into execution by the Assistant Provost of the 1st Division on the 2d January, 1811, in presence of the King's German Legion, at Albueras de Caixo, to be paraded for that purpose.

3. At a General Court Martial held by virtue of a warrant and in pursuance of an order from his Excellency Lieutenant

Lieutenant General Lord Viscount Wellington, K. B. Commander of the Forces, at Azambuja, 28th December, 1810, of which Major General the Honourable C. Colville was President, and Captain Goodman Deputy Judge Advocate, Private Martin Kiesing of the 1st Line Battalion King's German Legion, was arraigned for desertion on or about the 3d day of October, 1810;

To which charge the prisoner pleaded not guilty, and the Court having considered the evidence adduced in the prosecution against the prisoner, Private Martin Kiesing of the 1st Line Battalion King's German Legion, together with what he has submitted in his defence, are of opinion that he is guilty of the charge preferred against him, being in breach of the Articles of War, and do by virtue thereof sentence him to receive a punishment of One Thousand Lashes in the usual manner.

Which Sentence has been confirmed by this Excellency the Commander of the Forces.

4. Private Martin Kiesing is to be sent to his regiment, and the sentence of the General Court Martial is to be carried into execution by the Assistant Provost of the 1st Division on the 2d January, 1811, in presence of the King's German Legion, at Albueras de Caixo, to be paraded for that purpose.

5. The General Court Martial, of which Major General the Honourable Charles Colville is President, is adjourned, and the members are to return to their duty with their several brigades and regiments.

6. The Commander of the Forces requests that the Officers commanding regiments and of the artillery will report whether any soldier, or officer's servant, or driver of the artillery, or other person, who shall answer the following description,

description, was absent from his station during any part of the 24th instant, as a person of this description has committed a crime of the greatest magnitude.

DESCRIPTION.

Long visage, fair complexion, gray eyes, light hair cropped very short, apparently 25 or 26 years of age, had on a round hat with oil skin cover, blue jacket, and a pair of old blue stocking pantaloons.

INDEX.

INDEX.

VOL. II.

1810.

The Cavalry will continue to receive their ration as usual — — — 17

Feb. 2. Paymasters of regiments in the 1st Division to receive the balance on their estimates to 24th January — *ib.*

4. The General Court Martial of which Colonel the Hon. E. Stopford is president, ordered to reassemble on the 5th instant, is postponed until the 8th instant — *ib.*

14. Appointment of Hospital Mate Redford to act as Assistant Surgeon to the 45th regiment — — *ib.*

18. Sentence of a General Court Martial on privates P. Lang and G. Webby, 3d foot (or Buffs) — — 18

Appointment of Lieutenant Pemberton, 95th regiment, to act as A. D. C. to Brigadier General Campbell 19

Appointment of Captain the Hon. J. Stewart, 95th regiment, to act as Brigade Major — — *ib.*

19. Sentence of a General Court Martial on privates J. Benderman, F. Shoemaker and E. Kemp, 11th regiment *ib.*

Appointment of Captain Lord Clinton, 16th Light Dragoons, as Extra Aide-de-Camp to the Commander of the Forces — — 20

Appointment of Captain Anderson, Royal Fusileers, as Deputy Assistant Quarter Master General — *ib.*

Captain Rott, 2d battalion, 58th regiment, to place himself under the orders of Marshal Beresford — *ib.*

Appointment of Major General Picton and Staff *ib.*

Appointment of Major General the Hon. William Stewart and Staff — — — *ib.*

Men belonging to the Depot Squadron of the regiments of dragoons to be sent to Lisbon, Colonel Peacocke to report their arrival at Lisbon — — 21

Letters hitherto addressed to the Military Secretary, to be addressed to Captains Bouverie or Lord Fitzroy Somerset in the absence of the Military Secretary — *ib.*

20. Appointment of Captain B. Tripp, 11th regiment, as Deputy Assistant Adjutant General — — *ib.*

Appointment of Hospital Mate Thomas Hoey, as Assistant Surgeon to the Waggon Train — 22

The General Court Martial of which Colonel Peacocke is president is adjourned — — *ib.*

Sentence of a General Court Martial on private J. Overill, 61st regiment — — — 23

The Paymaster General to make an advance of 1500 dollars to each regiment on account of their estimates to the 24th instant — — — 24

22. Major General the Hon. G. L. Cole's Brigade to consist of the 27th, 40th and 97th regiments — — *ib.*

Major General Picton's do. do. 45th, 88th and 74th do. — — — *ib.*

The 3d Division to consist of Major General Picton's and Lightburn's brigades — — *ib.*

The 4th Division to consist of Major General Cole's and Brigadier General Campbell's brigade — *ib.*

1810.

the battle of Talavera de la Reyna, on the 27th and 28th days of July, 1809 — — — 35

House of Lords ——— } Returning thanks to House of Commons, 2d Feb. 1809, } the army for their distinguished conduct at the battle of Talavera de la Reyna, on the 27th and 28th days of July, 1809 36 to 40

Appointment of Captain Burgh as A. D. C. to the Commander of the Forces — — 40

6. The General Court Martial, of which Colonel the Hon. E. Stopford is President, is dissolved — — *ib.*

7. Appointment of J. L. Kemmington, and C. Bonomie, as Acting Assistant Commissaries — — *ib.*

Detail for a General Court Martial to assemble at Vizeu on the 12th instant — — — 41

10. Captain B. Tripp (D. A. A. G.) attached to the Cavalry Division — — — *ib.*

Captain W. Cotton (D. A. A. G.) attached to the 2d Division — — — *ib.*

13. Paymasters of regiments in the 3d, 4th, and Light Divisions of Infantry and the Hussars, to repair to Head Quarters for the purpose of receiving their balance due on their estimates to 24th February and 24th March — 42

14. Ordering Lieutenant Glascott, 16th Light Dragoons, to be placed in arrest for absenting himself without leave *ib.*

Ordering Captain Green, 61st regiment, from Lisbon to Head Quarters — — — *ib.*

15. Captain Campbell, 74th regiment (D. A. A. G.) resigns his situation on the Staff — — 43

Appointment of Serjeant C. Smyth, 45th regiment, as an Assistant Provost, attached to the 3d division *ib.*

16. Lieutenant Peacocke, 44th regiment, to place himself under the orders of Marshal Beresford — — *ib.*

17. A Board of Officers to assemble at the Commissary General's Stores on the 18th instant, to report on the state of stores and provisions esteemed damaged — *ib.*

Appointment of Major Lindsay, 39th regiment, Commandant of Detachments, vice Brevet Major Murphy, 88th regiment, resigned — — — *ib.*

18. Officers commanding regiments to make a return to the Quarter Master General of the number and state of the tents issued for the use of the Officers under the Orders of the 24th May last — — 44

Directing Mr. Gunson, Purveyor, to settle with the several regiments for the stoppages received out of the pay of soldiers sent into General Hospital under the General Order 14th September. After the 24th March no advance of pay is to be sent with the soldier to the General Hospital, referring to his Majesty's regulations, dated 31st March, and 30th April, 1800, on that head *ib.*

21. Directing returns of field equipment to be given in to the Quarter Master General agreeable to form — *ib.*

Regiments to send in to the Adjutant General returns of

 Officers

The

Captain

1810.

Apr. 29. Captain Cooke, Deputy Assistant Adjutant General, attached to the 4th Division, *vice* Captain Dashwood, Deputy Assistant Adjutant General, removed to the 1st Division — — — 68

Appointment of Serjeant Marshal, Coldstream Guards, as Post Master to the Army — — *ib.*

30. The Sick of the 3d, 4th, and Light Divisions, to be removed to Celerico on Thursdays, in lieu of Trancosa on Wednesdays — — — *ib.*

May 1. Appointment of Captain Lord James Hay, 4th West India Regiment, as Aide-de-Camp to Lieutenant General Sir S. Cotton — — — *ib.*

Appointment of Mr. Assistant Commissary Ogilvie to act as Deputy Commissary General to the 2d Division *ib.*

4. Regulations to be observed by the Commissariat and Paymaster General's Department in the conveyance of money from one station to another — 69

Major Crookshanks, 38th Regiment, to place himself under the orders of Marshal Beresford — 70

7. The Sick of the 1st, 3d, 4th, and Light Divisions, to assemble at Celerico every Thursday fortnight, in lieu of weekly, as directed by the Orders of the 30th ult. *ib.*

Directing Officers commanding regiments, to send in an account of sums stopped from the Soldiers for ammunition lost by neglect to the 24th of April last *ib.*

Appointment of Serjeant Eggleton, 4th Dragoons, as an Assistant Provost, *vice* Duval, deceased *ib.*

8. Captain Humphreys, 27th Regiment, Deputy Assistant Quarter-Master General, removed from the Staff of the Quarter-Master General's Department *ib.*

Appointment of Brevet Major Marston, 48th Regiment, as an Assistant in the Quarter-Master General's Department — — — *ib.*

Directing General Officers commanding Brigades, and Officers commanding Regiments of Cavalry, to adopt measures to prevent the Dragoons from selling the grain intended for the Cavalry Horses — 71

9. The General Court Martial, of which Major General Leith is President, is adjourned till further orders *ib.*

Detail for a General Court Martial to assemble at Portalegre — — — *ib.*

Detail for a General Court Martial to assemble at Lisbon on the 14th instant — — *ib.*

The Dragoons stationed for the conveyance of Dispatches are not to be sent with Letters except by an order from Head-Quarters, Lieutenant General Payne, &c. &c. 72

The usual Communication must be kept up by the Post, which passes through or near all the Quarters of the Army to and from Head-Quarters every day. Officers commanding at the different stations will take care to have a person at the proper place to receive their Letters *ib.*

1810.

1810.

Jun. 22. Sentence of a General Court Martial on Private James Maher, 57th Regiment — — 100

Private James Maher, 57th Regiment, to be sent a prisoner to Lisbon in irons — — *ib.*

Appointment of Captain Tucker, 29th Regiment, as Commandant of Detachments at Belem, *vice* Major Lindsay *ib.*

23. Paymasters of Regiments in the 3d and Light Divisions of Infantry, and the Hussars, to send to Almeida to receive the balance on their Estimates to the 24th of May 101

Paymasters of the other Cavalry Regiments, the 1st and 4th Divisions of Infantry, to send to Celorico for the balance on their Estimates to the 24th of May *ib.*

24. The Military Departments of Head-Quarters will move to Almeida to-morrow — — *ib.*

The Civil Departments of Head-Quarters will remain at Celorico — — — *ib.*

Regiments to send in Quarterly Returns of Officers who have been absent without leave during the preceding three months — — — *ib.*

Heads of Departments to transmit to the Adjutant General's Office, after the 25th instant, a List of Officers serving in their respective Departments, with a Memoranda, specifying all Appointments and Removals which have taken place during the preceding six months *ib.*

29. Head-Quarters will move to Alverca to-morrow 102

Appointment of the Generals and Staff Officers to serve with the Division of the Army stationed at Cadiz *ib.*

Captain W. Cotton, Deputy Assistant Adjutant General, attached to the Light Division, *vice* Graham 104

Appointment of Captain Radcliffe, Royal Dragoons, as Major of Brigade, *vice* Dance, resigned — *ib.*

Captain White, 3d Dragoon Guards, to place himself under the orders of Marshal Beresford — *ib.*

July 2. Appointment of Quarter Master Serjeant Stubbs, 31st regiment, as Assistant Provost Martial, *vice* Pass, resigned 105

Lieutenants Cheslyn and King, 48th Regiment, to place themselves under the orders of Marshal Beresford *ib.*

3. The General Court Martial, of which Colonel Saunders is President, is adjourned — — *ib.*

Colonel Saunders will remain at Lisbon until further orders *ib.*

Major Honourable A. Gordon, 3d Guards, is to resume his situation as extra Aide-de-Camp to the Commander of the Forces — — — *ib.*

Mr. Assistant Commissary General Ruth attached to the Cavalry Division — — *ib.*

List of Store Keepers discharged from the Commissariat Department — — — *ib.*

Paymasters

Detail

Hospital

To

 necessity

The

Directing

Lieut.

servants

Appoint-

Major

Captain

General

ERRATA.

Page 6, line 19, *for* 84th regiment, *read* 87th.
—— 61, line 13, *for* 14th April, *read* 15th.
—— 106, line 6, *for* Managan, *read* Monaghan.

London: Printed by C. Roworth, Bell Yard, Temple Bar.

www.ingramcontent.com/pod-product-compliance
Lightning Source LLC
LaVergne TN
LVHW010542160826
845677LV00013B/2962

* 9 7 9 8 9 8 5 5 5 6 6 3 6 *